Joël Desgrippes and Marc Gobé

on the Emotional Brand Experience

Written with Anne Hellman

Joël Desgrippes and Marc Gobé

on the Emotional Brand Experience

Written with Anne Hellman

BEVERLY MASSACHUSETTS

ROCKPORT PUBLISHERS

First published in the United States of America by
Rockport Publishers, a member of
Quayside Publishing Group
100 Cummings Center
Suite 406-L
Beverly, MA 01915
Telephone: (978) 282-9590
Fax: (978) 283-2742
www.rockpub.com

Library of Congress Cataloging-in-Publication Data available

ISBN-13: 978-1-59253-260-5
ISBN-10: 1-59253-260-8

10 9 8 7 6 5 4 3 2 1

Design: DesGrippes Gobé Group
Layout design: Leslie Haimes
Cover: Photographic collage by Marc Gobé.

Photographer Credits: Frédéric Berthet© clubmed, 95; Frédéric Berthet/Jean-Christophe Pratt© clubmed, 97 (top, second from left); Courtesy of Andrew Bordwin, 42–45; 47 (top & middle); 134 (bottom, right); 135 (middle); DesGrippes Gobé with Didier Lefort, 187, left (top & bottom); Courtesy of John Horner, 64–67; 198–199; Karine Laval/Jean-Christophe Pratt© clubmed, 96 (top); Anne Menoret, 56; 58; Bruno Van Loocke/Frédéric Berthet© clubmed, 97 (top, second from right); Déborah Metsch© clubmed, 97 (top right)

Package design 161; 162 (bottom) by Gragnani.

Printed in China

"It is only with the heart that one can see rightly.
What is essential is invisible to the eye."

—Antoine De Saint-Exupéry, *The Little Prince*

Contents

Introduction

Tell Me a Story: Emotional Branding and the Knack for Narrative

"I sometimes say that my job is to 'reveal personalities'. We want to give brands character and we want to give them meaning."—Joël Desgrippes

When, thirty-four years ago, Joël Desgrippes launched a "creative firm," as it was called then, little did he know that two of his natural talents—getting to know his clients personally and crafting captivating stories about their products—would one day help to inspire a new movement in the design world. When Marc Gobé joined on in 1980, he brought with him similar skills, gained from extensive design work in the beauty and fashion industries and in the United States. This is how Desgrippes Gobé quickly grew in two important ways: as a global entity with close ties to international clients, and as a profitable design firm that puts people's emotions first.

Desgrippes left the advertising business in 1971, foreseeing the rise of corporate ad agencies that had little or no connection to people, and started his own creative enterprise in Paris focused primarily on the beauty, fashion, and perfume trades. Here he was in his element; he made friends with artists, fashion designers, movie actors—celebrities of the highest echelon—and quickly began designing their beauty products for them. As his clients' businesses grew, he grew with them and expanded his enterprise into the international market. With Gobé onboard, the company opened an office in New York and subsequently in Brussels, Tokyo, Seoul, Hong Kong, and Shanghai.

What set Desgrippes Gobé apart from the outset was their natural ability to connect with clients. As early as 1980, they had devised a highly unique visual process called SENSE® to define a brand's emotional persona. They used the SENSE® process to create stories around major fragrance and cosmetics brands they were working with at the time because these products had nothing tangible to sell. The stories added an emotional dimension that customers could grab onto, leave the store with, and appreciate at home. This was the foundation of the philosophy that now underscores everything Desgrippes Gobé does, and as established by Marc Gobé's best selling book, a new paradigm in the branding-design world: *emotional branding.*

Just as Desgrippes Gobé's signature brand narratives helped bridge the gap between the esoteric qualities of a fragrance and the consumer, emotional branding is the bridge between corporations and consumers in today's marketplace. Gobé, in his 2000 book titled *Emotional Branding* (Allworth Press), emphasizes the human connections between corporations and consumers: "Emotional branding is more than a process or research technique; it is based on the connections between people that transcend charts and graphs. It is a culture and a way of living; a fundamental belief that people are the real force in commerce and that business and the street cannot survive separately."

Long before many other design firms (and there weren't that many when Desgrippes Gobé started out) conceived of the necessity of making contact with consumers, not just "impacting" them with loud visual graphics and a thunderous corporate presence, Desgrippes Gobé based its entire strategy on this concept. From its inception, the firm believed that the creative force behind a company was just as important as its marketing force. The notion of a business fueled by creativity, by design, was entirely new at the time; in fact, Joël Desgrippes was the first to term the phrase "marketing design" and to realize it in the operations of his own firm.

It was this idea of *contact* versus *impact* that crystallized Desgrippes Gobé's design vision and showed companies around the world what they were missing out on. "The most important aspect is the individual, the human being," Desgrippes insists. "A human being has a passport, an ID card, things that are tangible—blue eyes, a certain age—and these things don't change. Then of course there is something much more important, which is the personality of the individual. And of course this personality can change, can move; it gets married, gets divorced, has children. The brand is the same thing. That's where we really work hard on brands: their personalities."

The firm has developed other tools like SENSE®, such as Brand Focus and the Brand Management System, to gain a complete understanding of their client, their client's aspirations for the brand, and the sensory elements that can be leveraged through design to bring about a lasting connection between brand and consumer. Today, the firm's expertise spans the gamut of brand building, from brand strategy—positioning, brand architecture, new product development—to brand design—logo, emotional identity systems, packaging—to environmental design and digital branding.

As Marc Gobé and I talked at his New York office one humid September afternoon, I glance at images of recent Desgrippes Gobé projects spread out on the thick glass table between us. My eye catches the vibrant red of Coca-Cola's revamped packaging graphics; the cool, familiar, but somehow different, blue of AOL's new logo; colorful, eye-popping packaging for the Kenzo Jungle fragrance; the fleshlike lines of a Victoria's Secret perfume bottle. Gobé tells me that he found his inspiration in nature growing up on a farm in western France and that he has an equal fascination with urban environments and the richness of culture expressed in them. He talks about how human nature is at the core of everything: it beats beneath the surface of what we do like a great big, constantly thumping heart. When we express ourselves, every word we choose to speak, every article of clothing we choose to wear, every product we choose to buy—all of these are various manifestations of our true nature.

Design manifests itself through people. Urban dwellers pulse with the hyper-concentration of culture that only a city environment can produce. Here humanity is expressed in cell-phone accessories, high-heel shoes, a pair of jeans, the glass curve of a building or shop interior. All of these things relate back to human nature. In order to make contact, you've got to go to the source.

"It is rare that we create identities that are locked up, that don't inspire," says Gobé, tracing a finger along the company's impressive range of images. Perhaps this is why, as I sift through the Desgrippes Gobé designs, my gaze lingers on the hand-painted feel of the logo for Musashino University in Japan, on the gestural sketches for the 1992 Albertville Winter Olympics, on the colorful, sinuous lettering of the Crédit Agricole emblem, the sensuous, ribbonlike curve running down

the Coca-Cola can. I begin to see it: the "hand" behind the design, the designer's touch that gives Desgrippes Gobé creations their humanistic, spontaneous feel and in turn shapes a corporate identity into an emotional one. I watch as brands transform, literally before my eyes, into presences, personalities that will be there for their customers, open to their needs, helping them to express themselves.

My eyes finally come to rest on the sparkling new uniform for the Rakuten Eagles, a Japanese baseball team, shown in photos sent over from the firm's Tokyo office. Emblazoned across the chest of the white jersey is the team name, fanning out on either end like a pair of wings. The *E* at the beginning of *Eagles* and the *S* at its end look strikingly like

Japanese characters. The Japanese-style E is repeated on the cap. Even the "1" in the player's number incorporates the look of Japanese lettering. The team name appears to be about to fly off the jersey, while the blend of Japanese and Western characters anchors it in its cultural context: this is a Japanese baseball team, and baseball is a Western sport. What is most noticeable is the way neither the Japanese identity nor the Western one disappears; both are present in the design. Gobé describes the design as a "synergy" of two cultures; neither identity is lost in the mix.

This notion of an inspired connection between different cultures, as that between a brand identity and its customer, is of utmost importance to the Desgrippes Gobé vision. It is a concept that comes naturally to a firm that from its inception grounded itself in a global identity, that aimed—years before other agencies saw the need—to infuse design with humanity itself. Every Desgrippes Gobé office works to transform the entire brand experience, from product design to packaging to retail environment to product development. In all its worldly manifestations, the firm aims to show the consistency of the human element throughout its designs and environments, to craft, ultimately, the *emotional brand experience.*

"That's what emotional branding is: it is creating a strong, affectionate relationship between the consumer and the brand," explains Desgrippes. This is why Desgrippes Gobé pens hand-drawn forms with lots of color and builds warm, vibrant environments. They steer clear of scholarly, academic interpretations and follow their gut instincts, listening so closely to what a brand has to say they can hear the story inside waiting to be told.

Anne Hellman

Meet Marc Gobé / "Visual Anthropologist"

Q: In what ways did your background help to define you as a designer?

A: I was brought up on a farm in the west of France and I was a very active boy at the time, so during vacation I would help out. My father was a cattle trader, and we could also fish and hunt on the farm. I would help cut and gather the hay and the wheat, and everyone who helped out ate together outside. It was this incredible experience. Most important, it was extremely sensorial in terms of being around animals and nature. I have a really strong love of sensorial things. I can recognize a scent. I loved working in those fields. In other words, I have always loved nature; I'm not afraid of nature. Things like bugs and snakes, those things have never bothered me; it's part of what life is.

When I went into the design business, I always felt that the relationships that people had with brands were based on the fact that those products and those packagings, those creations, needed to be sensorial, needed to be experiential, needed to help people discover something about themselves, something that they hadn't experienced before. Because of the way I grew up, I have a tremendous respect for nature and for the human balance. I always connect the world of design with how it affects the environment, how it affects people. That's why when we talk about examples like the nature wall in Tokyo, this is something that excites me because it is a perfect partnership between people and nature. And we are only at the beginning.

I think brands are about democracy, because I come from a country (France) that has seen, since the Second World War, a tremendous explosion in its economy and trading, opportunities for people to find work and to express themselves. Suddenly, we were exposed to brands, international brands, and it seemed like we were traveling in the world before we actually started traveling. This is a huge factor that has defined my personality and my fascination with and love of brands. I'm always engaged emotionally in what I do because I have a strong sense of this.

I call myself a "visual anthropologist." I always have a camera with me, and I love to take photos of signage, because the typographics of a country are the best expression of its culture. I take photos of people, because I think people say a lot about a particular culture—what they are wearing, the way they look, how they express themselves. Sometimes this is a source of ideas for product development. I have series of photos on materials, faces, and food markets around the world. To me it's always an inspiration. It shows me that life is always evolving; it doesn't stay in the same place. As the branding cycles keep on changing, the best source of insight is observing people, because you see how the culture is evolving and where different cultures are going, how they express themselves, and how that could affect design.

Q: How did you first meet Joël Desgrippes?

A: I met Joël at an advertising agency in France, where we both worked as art directors. I left France to travel around the world, went to Asia, and ran out of money in San Francisco, and so I needed to find a job. I found a job at a company called Botsford Ketchum, and they hired me to manage the UTA French airlines account, which is an airline that doesn't exist anymore but which mostly specialized in trips from France to Africa and in the U.S. in trips from Los Angeles to Tahiti. I worked on their campaign for a year and was lucky to have found an agency that had a French account. This was 1970. After a year, in order to stay in the country—and I wanted to do that—I had to get a visa, and in order to get a visa at the time I had to start a business.

My experience in San Francisco was interesting because I worked with the wine industry, with brands like Christian Brothers in Napa. I also created my first major logo, which was for a railroad company called Western Pacific. It was really exciting for

me to see it on the boxcars of the trains as they went by. The logo was a feather, because the railroad transported technology, things that were precious, fragile, and that needed to be treated "lightly."

At the time, Joël was on vacation in San Francisco and asked me to become a partner in the design firm he had started in Paris. I went back to Paris for about five years, where part of my responsibility was to develop the U.S. market, and after five years I was spending two weeks a month in New York just to manage the accounts in America. I liked it so much that I wanted to come back and open an office in New York, a Desgrippes Gobé office. Subsequently, we later opened offices in Seoul, Tokyo, Hong Kong, Shanghai, and then Brussels. So, the core of the partnership, from the very beginning, had an international component. It really was global in its heart.

Q: Were you one of the first design firms to think globally?

A: There were some firms that were already there but not many, so we were probably among the group of five firms that really took branding and design internationally. What made the company a really interesting company right off the bat was the fact that we had this international perspective.

Q: Also the fact that you were designers. Weren't design firms relatively new at that time?

A: Design firms were an emerging trend at that point. We've taken the international perspective further over the years. For example, when we were designing the new graphics for the packaging and branding of Coca-Cola, we invited the offices from Paris and Tokyo to join in on the initial meeting, and the perspectives that people had on the brand, coming from different places, were extremely influential on the process. I have to give credit to our Tokyo office for helping bring back the Dynamic Ribbon, which was a graphic that spoke volumes about the culture, more so than the contour bottle, which was the graphic on the can at the time and was perceived as a little old-fashioned.

So our company culture was constantly enriched by those inspirations. The other country offices were picking up on what the Paris and New York offices were doing, and building and creating designs that were consistent with the whole philosophy.

Q: Is that something that you strive for, to have all of your offices keep up a similar aesthetic?

A: We meet as a limited group of executives a few times a year, and we meet again once a year for planning the vision of the company. We privilege the business side of what we are doing as much as we do the design side. Before, there was no cooperation between the two. We wanted creativity but also we wanted to build a company that could grow, that financially could attract the best people, be credible in front of large clients and capable of handling global programs, and to do it profitably.

Q: You must be attractive to larger companies who are looking for something new, something less corporate than what the bigger firms produce.

A: We've been able to keep the image of a boutique shop, but one with global expertise. And since we never compromised on the creative process, it allowed us to always be sought after by clients that needed new responses, new visions, a new design

approach, something that was a bit subversive. We always attracted clients who wanted to go beyond the existing formulas and who really believed in design. I think that one of the criteria of the best client relationships is that, each time, the client believed in design, believed in the power of the creative process and trusted it. They considered designers to be the real creative resources to inspire their business.

When I started the business in the United States I had the good fortune of working with Les Wexner of The Limited at a time when he was creating new brands such as Express, Bath & Body Works, and Victoria's Secret. As a merchant and as a highly creative person and curious mind, he gave us the opportunity to take our design capabilities beyond what we did before that. He was in a way the first one who gave us the opportunity to work not only on a logo or packaging, but also on store design and product development. So as one of the people that truly understood the power of the imagination and design, he raised the image of the company and gave us the self-confidence to carry out the same type of vision with other clients. He indirectly transformed the group into what it is today and was one of the people who helped to shape our philosophy.

Q: In your process of taking photographs in different places, of objects and people, do you find inspiration in both rural and urban environments? Do you ever venture outside of the city into nature itself and take photographs, or are you looking more at people in densely populated areas?

A: There is a magic in the urban construct. It's where a country's culture is expressed the most intensely. It's where we can come up with a sort of logic of how people live and how commerce is embedded in those formats. And then out in nature, because this is where there is some profound natural truth, that's where you find the origin, the core, of everything that's going to be expressed in the city, the sensorial aspects, the textures, the colors. You can get inspired by the shapes of stones, how the snow carves its way into a mountain—or even just feeling the wind in your face brings about a sensory experience, an energy that emotionally you want to translate into brands. When connecting to brands, people are also connecting to a different reality that is inspiring and transforming.

Q: And that really is the foundation of emotional branding.

A: My first book, *Emotional Branding,* one of the first to talk about the importance of emotions in brands, was a reflection of the major influence this new paradigm we had developed was having on the branding world. Compared to some of the books that had come before it, my book was not academic. It talked about my experiences working with brands from a visceral perspective and told personal stories that have shaped my perception of what brands need to be, and how brands are sometimes missing the important factor, which is that they have to bring joy into people's lives. And that really is what emotional branding is about; it's not only about branding but about being humanistic. I can't disconnect brands from human life and their environment because I really do believe that they are an expression of life and society.

Q: Almost like an art form, in a sense.

A: Like anything that we find in nature or in life, it could become an art form. I like to take photos of cities, because cities transform themselves to be an art form. Even when you go to the *favelas* in Brazil, for instance, it's amazing how people bring a new layer of personalization, even in the worst situations, to reach a sense of dignity.

Q: In a way, you're talking about branding as something that filters through humans and becomes an expression of humanity. Do you think that's an indication that something is shifting? Are we changing as a world, as a people; are we able to express ourselves more freely?

A: I think that the postmodern world that we're living in—which is really starting to be the full expression of democracy in a way, supports the concept of individuality. This new trend toward individuality is the single most profound change that we are able to see in this century, where the sense of personal self-expression and the freedom to stand out as an individual, even if part of a group, is probably the most inspiring thing that brands are still trying to capture. Democracy that leads to freedom at the same time encourages people to express that freedom; in the context of a society, people's lives become their personal projects. And the fun in finding ways to express one's personality has also been an opportunity for brands to provide experiences, products, or services that help people to be more involved.

The perception of branding is different in countries that have more history as freemarkets than emerging countries have. In emerging markets, people see brands as a symbol of progress because they have not been able to access brands or even buy brands, so when they do have the ability to buy brands it means that their society is evolving, it means that there is hope for the future, that there are jobs around the corner, and a better life for them and their families and their children. And at the same time, when those brands do a good job, they help them express something about their new reality. In Mexico, for instance, brands like The Body Shop, with its strong stance on violence against women, become subtle messages to share. Other brands give you the message that it's okay to be independent and expressive, and that freedom of choice is around the corner—because freedom of choice is imperative to brands.

Q: The brand, then, represents a person's personality in some way.

A: It can help. It can help bring self-esteem to people. It can help people send out messages about who they are. When I design, or when I think about design, I seek out the optimistic, personal, memorable, and at the same time more intuitive ways of expressing brands so that people feel comfortable with them and endorse them as part of their lives, as something that really drives them.

Q: The company also benefits, doesn't it? The consumer gets all of these things, but can't the brand also represent the company's personality?

A: We were living in a world where corporations believed that they could regulate people's consumption habits to fit a particular production model. This was the age of mass marketing. There was very little passion for creating products that could fit into people's lifestyles. Products were generic and commoditized. This model went against people's individual desire for experiences and it started weakening the personality of leading brands. At that time, design had a functional role: to facilitate production. It was not a brand building tool.

Consumers were at the opposite end of this model, looking to learn more, hear more, and feel more as Susan Sontag so eloquently said. In a post-modern economy where people's individual choices and emotional experiences were key to brand building, corporations were slow to change their production model.

Desgrippes Gobé saw those fundamental changes in society and believed that we would move from generic products to products that would stimulate people's experiences with the brands. In our opinion, design would be the new message and a competitive point of difference between brands. Because of our work in the fashion and beauty industries, we believed that design could help make a positive emotional connection between a brand and its consumers.

Q: And you established that as an idea very early on in the company?

A: This was in 1980, so yes, it was a very new idea and a powerful idea at the time, when we believed that the way brands expressed themselves in a personal way would help the success of those brands. Suddenly what we were thinking of was really a partnership between what was perceived as a disconnected process of design and the business objectives of corporations.

We were also one of the first firms to coin the term "strategic design," which was our way of bridging the gap between the logical reality of the business world and a different reality, which was the emotional reality of the consumers: we were not looking at brands in the way corporations did, as money-making propositions only, we were looking at brands as life-enhancing experiences.

Such brands as Nike, Starbucks, or Apple, because of their success in defining emotional narratives around their brand, started to support those kinds of messages. We were right there. I remember in 1982, a team of Apple designers came to see us in Paris. They came to talk to us about design, about emotional design. They were very curious about what we were doing in the beauty world. So already from the beginning they were thinking about design, about how their design could impact culture.

When we worked in the beauty industry, we had to create narratives for the brands. Fragrances, for instance, don't have a strongly differentiated offering except through the olfactory experience. Packaging and storytelling then become the elements that will support a fragrance's success. What makes this more difficult is that consumer research that has been conducted about fragrances has never been conclusive, so it's all about the narrative and all about the emotions that it creates. It's a way to make brands connect with people by placing them right at the center of people's emotional lives, by giving them the tools to help them feel different about themselves. A fragrance can be perceived as either sexy, beautiful, or fresh, but most importantly, it empowers someone to be noticed, whether that person be a lover, a friend, or an acquaintance.

The fashion industry is fascinating in a different way because unlike any other business it has to renew itself every single season, and in order to do that designers have to rely on their instincts to imagine what their customers will buy. They have to be connected to those customers and they have to be ahead of the customer's choices. Of course, you can't ask the customer what they want. How could you? You are creating fashion styles that don't exist yet, even in their wildest imaginations. It's an industry that relies on design inspiration and instinct to succeed, and this is a process that we have always been familiar with and that we try to emulate in the partnerships with our clients.

Design can become a source of inspiration, a vision, and an emotional experience. Design is about life, truth, beauty, and sensory experiences. I find this inspiration in the roots of my heritage, in the harmonic expression of nature, and in life. Maybe it is because I am still a farmer at heart that I am able to observe the power of nature expressing itself in the most magnificent way. Now I use design as an extension of the lessons I have discovered in the logic of nature. Design is a process of discovery and inspiration that continues to blossom in our mind as it stimulates our imagination and our senses around new ideas.

Meet Joël Desgrippes / "Theatrical Director"

Q: Marc Gobé calls himself a "visual anthropologist." Do you have a word or sentence to describe yourself and your work?

A: My profession is close to that of a theatrical director. We make brands come alive and give them meaning. With us brands become stars; we give them a theatricalness. We create a specific world for each brand; we relocate them into their environment. We give them a vision.

Q: How did you get interested in design? Was there something in your life that led you to becoming a designer?

A: I think I'm just an inventive spirit. Creativity is related to a constant search for innovation and new ways of living. What first attracted me to design was a real passion for new ideas. I also wanted to create a profession with my own vision and put all my talent at the consumer's service. Design is life. It is also about making everyday life more pleasant.

Q: What was your career like before you created your design firm?

A: I graduated from the Arts Graphiques School at the top of my class. This school was a revelation for me and opened my eyes to creative professions. I learned everything about the communication professions and this really helped me in my first illustration job. I worked in the literary field and then worked on film credits for the Beatles but also for *La Belle et la Bête (Beauty and the Beast)* for Jean Marais.

These were my first experiences before working in the advertising world as a creative director. During the first three years of my career, I was lucky to be entrusted with creating major advertising campaigns. I also participated in Dubonnet and Triumph billboard campaigns and the launch of 1664 for Kronenbourg. That was my very first packaging experience. At the time, these first jobs triggered my understanding and passion for fashion and luxury products.

It was also at this point in my professional life that I understood that it was essential to build a bridge between marketing and design. Although it was obvious to me, it was a very new vision in the seventies because we were just beginning to use these techniques in France. I coined the phrase "marketing design" to designate the absolute need for strategic thought combined with creativity.

I left the advertising world in the seventies when I realized that ad agencies were becoming large international financial groups. I thought that the size of these agencies would not allow me to maintain my personality and my independence. So I created my own agency.

Q: So you had to invent the "design profession"?

A: That was true at the time; you had to be a visionary to pursue a career in design. The profession did not exist—no one talked about design. I had to invent the work on the brand, the product, and its presentation in distribution based on pure intuition.

Q: What was it called then?

A: It was usually called a "creative office." Nobody spoke of design. Only Raymond Loewy, with all his talent, spoke about design with great passion. He is my inspiration.

At the time there were only a few of us, and the profession was not as structured as it is today. I believe I contributed greatly to the development and professionalism of this field. In fact I have been President of the ADC (Association of French Design Agencies) for many years.

Q: Tell us about the early days of the Desgrippes agency. How has your outlook on the profession and your methodology changed?

A: At first I began by creating mainly products for the luxury and perfume industry. At the time I met many celebrities and that is how I started to work for them and move in the fashion and cinema world. I worked directly with Bernard Lanvin, Catherine Deneuve, Omar Sharif, Alain Delon, Stéphanie de Monaco, Gianfranco Ferré, the Ferragamo family, and the very beginning of Prada in the fashion world. I was also good friends with Claude François, who owned a press group and a modeling agency. Meeting these people led me to think about identity and brand issues. How to build a consistent world based on these personalities, especially in the perfume field—a strategic consideration and approach to the product and brand.

Then I became interested in mass distribution and service companies. In 1988 we created the Crédit Agricole logo, which hasn't changed since. Later it seemed evident to focus on new media like the Internet.

It is fundamental in this profession to remain as close as possible to consumer expectations. At the beginning of the eighties, Marc and I worked on the "Chic et Choc" distribution concept for the RATP (Paris Transportation Authority). Selling a whole collection of objects in stores located on the Paris subway network was a truly innovative concept. It was a real break with traditional distribution and the first time that an institutional brand gave birth to products. We sold tableware, posters, stationery, etc. We created hundreds of objects. This helped to valorize the RATP brand and especially make the Paris subway something more pleasant and accessible to all.

I also realized at this time that mass distribution had everything to learn from selective distribution and, conversely, that selective distribution had everything to learn from mass distribution. Today we work in three main professions: the brand, the product, and distribution. It is what we call branding. It is a transversal consideration of the three main problems facing our clients and applies to every type of distribution. Today the boundary between luxury products and mass products is almost invisible. The differences must be handled with subtlety.

Q: Product - brand - distribution, how does design fit into these three fundamentals?

A: Every day you have to ask three big questions:

How do you feed the brand to give it life?
How do you create innovative products that become part of the brand history?
How do you bring the brand and products to life through distribution?

That is the essence of our work.

But everything starts with a big brand idea that we call "the vision" and that we have made real with "Design is vision."

Q: Has the sensitivity you developed in luxury marketing allowed you to refine this "emotional branding" vision?

A: Yes, of course, because in luxury marketing everything is suggested—nothing is truly explicit. It is a world of sensitivity. Everything is subliminal in this world: the fragrance conveyed by the bottle, the creator's vision by the shape, material, feel, colors, even the sound of the object. It is through these various considerations that we have understood the identity dimension of the brand and the other, much more subtle, facet of the brand: the imaginary. This aspect best allows us to express the brand's personality and vision. It is all about balance, contrast but also about complementarity. This is where the strength and versatility of our creativity lies.

Q: Can you tell us how this consideration was made real in your work on the Air France brand?

A: It is true that for Air France the work on brand perception levels was fundamental. We carried out an extremely in-depth exploration of this brand to identify and adapt our proposals to the many different media and facets the brand uses to express itself. Some media must remain identity-based, while others can draw on the imaginary that this great French brand can offer.

A brand is alive and must continue evolving over time without losing its identity. It is hand-crafted, like fine jewelry, and probably the most interesting part of our profession. To accomplish this we need many in-house talents. Few agencies have this sensitivity and I must pay tribute to all the talents surrounding me as they allow us to stand out when compared to other design agencies.

Q: Marc told me that you are very interested in interior architecture design. Is this the field that best allows you to express your knowledge?

A: In our profession we always have a 2D and 3D approach. 2D affects only part of our brain and imagination. When you think 3D you think in terms of space, light, movement, volume, etc. You are no longer outside the creation—you are in it, you participate in the space and all of your senses are awakened.

The other point of view is purely architectural, an art form that I especially like. We are involved in what lasts, a significant gesture that marks an era, a time. It is the widest range expression of what can be implemented for a brand. Design is a complex and rich profession. I love it.

Q: Is Desgrippes Gobé's work a means of gaining access to the brand's personality?

A: The personality is in fact an essential aspect of our profession. Design gives meaning to what we create. Aesthetics alone do not interest me. We reveal personalities.

Everything can be communicated by design, we go for the essence. We create affective links between the brand and the consumer. Everything communicates via design, a product, architecture, image, etc. This is why I consider design to be a profession of personalization and differentiation.

It's almost a human vision of the brand . . .

The human being is the most important thing in the world. But behind the physical being there is an individual's personality which makes every being different and exceptional as such. This is what we try to express with the brand. A human being has a passport, an identity card. They describe age, size, nationality and eye color; they are tangible and irreversible things. But behind these irrefutable elements there is an individual's life, and of course this may change and evolve. People marry, have children, divorce— they create a family and a history.

Brands are the same: they live, they change, join partnerships, separate, create subsidiaries, adapt to their environment, and are enriched by different experiences and cultures. This is our daily work.

Of course, like any relationship with an individual, one has feelings, specific affections. This is what we are trying to create: attachment, particular links between the brand and the consumer. We want to give personalities to brands and meaning to their lives.

Q: How does this influence your methodologies? Is this why relationships are so important in your profession?

A: Knowing a client's personality and being able to conceive of the imaginary that brings life and personality are key elements of our work.

Desgrippes Gobé owes the concept of "emotional branding" to our first jobs in the perfume field and in the fashion and beauty world. There are no truths in this world. None of the studies that have been carried out in this field have successfully analyzed all the subtleties regarding consumer attachment to these brands. This attachment is only made up of the emotions that the brands inspire. It is the art of creating a relation-based link with the individual and placing brands at the heart of the person's life.

We can't please everyone. We have to be able to choose and remain constant and loyal to a strategy. And we always have to surprise. This is essential for luxury brands.

Q: Is there a Desgrippes Gobé "house spirit"?

A: Yes. I believe that like any great house there is a Desgrippes Gobé spirit. But beyond this style and philosophy, the object that we design must belong to the brand and reflect the vision of the company and the person for which we create it. That is what has made us famous. We are the very expression of the brands for which we create. We disappear completely behind these brands and are always very discreet in our work. This is in fact a generalist profession centered on the personality of each brand in order to open all possible paths to allow the brand to reveal itself in the most true and beautiful sense.

Q: You have developed close relationships with some of your clients?

A: I cannot work with a creator without knowing his/her personality, tastes or differences. Our clients all have very different, very set personalities.

I am a professional in the field of creativity. I am not an artist; I like to disappear behind the client. We are the expression of the brands for which we work and not the expression of ourselves. The Desgrippes Gobé agency was built on the sensitivity to the artistic and industrial worlds. It is only after working with them over a long period that today we are able to fully express ourselves.

Q: You seem attached to the idea of multiculturalism.

A: I have a strong belief in mixing cultures, in their differences and also what brings them together. Every voyage is enriching to me. It is important to know how to look, listen, and understand. I feed on the street. It is enriching for me, and of course my clients benefit directly from it.

I don't like the word "globalization." I'm interested only in the international dimension. I'm against standardizing and leveling. I think that the European environment, the wealth of French history and that of Europe contribute a certain sensitivity and openness that enrich our professions. The cultural heritage in France and in Europe gave birth to and has greatly contributed to international creative trends.

It is important to remember that in France, for example, 60 percent of the industrial context is made up of small- and medium-sized companies. French craftsmanship and know-how is recognized worldwide. Tableware, glass making, embroidery, and leather goods are steady references. These small companies cover all the know-how of the creative world, and they are now oriented toward industrializing their know-how. This cultural fabric is an extraordinary heritage which is present in the international collective unconscious and gives a real economic reality to our country. We French are sometimes too discreet.

Q: Today you are an international agency. What led to the necessary internationalization of your agency?

A: When I started I was mostly based in Paris. I often traveled to Italy because the fashion world is based there and I found it to be a very fertile ground for expression. Along with France, it is a place where fashion finds a great deal of inspiration and talent.

When our clients began to open up to increasingly international markets, I understood that I had to enlarge my company and give it a more international dimension. At the time, clients wanted to enter the American and Asian markets.

I went to the United States—without being able to speak a word of English—to contact the players in the perfume field, and I had the wonderful opportunity to meet Estée Lauder, a bigger-than-life personality. Estée Lauder was my first client in the United States.

That is also when Marc and I decided to become partners and really develop in the United States. I had met him in advertising in France, and at that time in his life he wanted to move to the United States, and this is why we formed our partnership. This was the first major international step for the Desgrippes Gobé agency, and we then opened offices in Asia and expanded our presence in Europe. Today we have seven D/G offices in the world, and we collaborate with international know-how networks to propose a range of solutions that are complementary to our in-house resources.

Q.: Why do you think that it is important for a branding design company especially, such as Desgrippes Gobé, to be an international organization? How do you think this influences your work in design?

A: Today, creative professions must have an international dimension. There is a real international culture which is enriched by confronting various cultures: Japanese, Chinese, European, or American. These cultural differences lead to different consumption modes that imply different ways of experiencing brands and designing products. Without knowing these different cultures, it is impossible to create international products.

Q.: Although Desgrippes Gobé is a large company—ranked as the sixth largest global design group—it has a human dimension with a strong in-house corporate culture. Does this organization and strong identity help you in your international development?

A: In fact, we have the right dimension internationally today because we are present on three continents. Our image as a large company is recognized throughout the world. It gives us our own personality and differentiates us from other design agencies.

Every day, this combination of a large international company operating as a small structure helps us to maintain our sensitivity and our proximity while being able to reason on a global scale. It is because we provide sensitivity to brands and through years of work that we have obtained this legitimacy. Our capacity for capturing the hard-to-define subtleties specific to the luxury and perfume worlds have led us to professionalizing our sensibility and giving it a real character. Marc Gobé explains this very well in his book *Emotional Branding*.

Q.: On a personal level, what are your passions?

A: In addition to my professional travels around the world, I am also interested in African art, contemporary painting, and gardens. I spend a lot of time and energy on my passions. They are real sources of vitality and creativity for me. For example, right now I am creating a multicultural garden in which I structure the space and create links between the different types of gardens. It is the same thing I do in my profession every day.

Q.: How were you raised? How did your education influence you?

A: I grew up in Maisons-Laffitte, a small town west of Paris known for raising racehorses. The proximity to Paris helped me to discover the city and the world of fashion and perfume. This is when I discovered my taste for the creative field.

In Maisons-Laffitte I also basked in another aesthetic—that of horse-raising and the world of men who try to tame the power in this magnificent and majestic animal, a real "mechanical marvel," very well designed.

Q.: Did you draw as much inspiration from this natural environment as you did in the city? Was there something there that inspired you?

A: It is true that living outside of Paris while being close to it provided me with environmental contrasts and balance. The difference between the quick pace of the city and the fact that I lived outside that world helped open my mind to the interplay of contrasts, imbalances, and contradictions. It is a way of thinking that I identify with; I believe that the point of confrontation is where things happen.

I am always looking for the dichotomy between shape and its opposite, light and shadow. In our profession when you disturb things, when you make things move, this is when real ideas appear.

The Desgrippes Gobé Methodology

Desgrippes Gobé has cultivated three methodological tools for heightening a brand's emotional resonance with consumers. Implementing these tools in the branding process means the difference between simply creating another marketing emblem and generating a life for the brand based on its human qualities and connections with people. Developed exclusively by Desgrippes Gobé, each tool is unique to the firm's innovative approach of emotional branding.

1. Brand Focus

"A man always has two reasons for the things he does: a good reason, and a real reason." —J.P. Morgan

Translated in branding language as: "People buy things for two reasons, the right reason: logic, and the real reason: emotion."

In order to help a brand create emotion, and therefore meaning and memory, Desgrippes Gobé first goes to the source—to the company vision behind the brand. Brand Focus is an interactive consulting tool that helps a company's management team align itself with a heartfelt brand vision. Desgrippes Gobé conducts Brand Focus sessions with the team to clarify a brand's positioning and unveil its potential to communicate beyond its current message.

Step One: Information Gathering

To initiate the Brand Focus process, Desgrippes Gobé meets with the company's management team to get a briefing on the project and to discuss specific concerns, considerations, and parameters for the development of the brand vision. By interviewing top executives, project directors, and employees, the team explores the company's internal business strategy as well as its essential spirit and culture. The brand's lifecycle—from creation to evolution to repositioning to re-launch and back to creation—is analyzed to clarify challenges ahead.

By conducting either one large session with the client or several separate sessions for each corporate contingent, the Desgrippes Gobé team gathers data that can then be fed into a single, cohesive strategy that is both relevant and meaningful.

Step Two: The Brand Focus Exercise

Brand Focus is played much like an interactive game, which encourages brainstorming and helps the client to unearth a whole range of unfiltered viewpoints. These flesh out the hidden nuances behind the brand that can be expanded upon in creative and strategic ways.

First, Desgrippes Gobé defines several visual categories, displaying a series of images that represent a range of attitudes and styles, all of which could easily represent the brand. The team assesses the images and selects those cues that represent the brand's unique point of view. The chosen images are then used to craft a brand portrait, and the words and vocabulary are used to rationalize the image choices as well as open up crucial brand-opportunity discussions.

This first visual exercise defines the "state of the team." The visuals that are shown immediately incite either positive or negative reactions to determine the strengths and weaknesses of the brand. Other categories and visuals are

WORLD GOLF
VILLAGE

presented along with questions such as: If (brand) were a ride—what would it feel like? If (brand) were a wedding—what kind would it be? If (brand) were a dream vacation—where would it be?

The second part of the exercise focuses on the identification of core brand attributes that will support the visual voice created through the previous image exercise. An adjective brainstorm is conducted to explore a variety of meanings associated with the brand. These are recorded, and at the end of the image game, each participant is asked to pull three words from the board that define the essence of the brand. Desgrippes Gobé then synthesizes the selected visuals and attributes into a brand-positioning platform.

The result of the exercise is a focused brand-positioning expression communicated both visually and verbally. Based on the positioning, Desgrippes Gobé outlines programs for brand development and communication and pinpoints key cultural trends and opportunities in the market and beyond. The final

Brand Focus presentation is a multisensory report that can be used internally by the company to brief creative agencies and serve as a foundation for brand-image programs in the future.

The Head, Heart, Gut Framework

One vital result of the Brand Focus process is to humanize a brand. What connections does it make? Where do the disconnections exist? Ultimately, the question is: Where does the brand move the consumer most—in the head, the heart, or the gut? Desgrippes Gobé has designed a Head, Heart, Gut framework to determine a brand's different contact points with the consumer and whether these match up with consumer expectations. On one end of the trajectory are the consumer's "head" expectations, which are concerned with the brand's rational attributes. On the other end are the imaginative "heart" and "gut" expectations, related to the brand's social interactions and visceral and intuitive connections.

Desgrippes Gobé classifies each point of contact within the Head, Heart, Gut framework to determine how a brand communicates with its target audience and to envision the optimal way of doing so. The team creates a visual territory, or system of visual elements, for each of the Head, Heart, and Gut emotional levels. The visual system it develops for the "head" communications includes any communication in which the identification of the brand is of primary importance, such as signage and sales publications. Here Desgrippes Gobé centers the visuals around core identity items such as logo and color palette.

For the "heart" communications, Desgrippes Gobé emphasizes the humanistic side of the brand, its unique personality, and the socially responsible role it plays though the brand elements that interact most closely with the consumer, such as the physical retail space and the company website. "Gut" communications are expressed through more sensory experiences that are invisible and instinctual and that have to be communicated on a purely subconscious level, including retail atmosphere, design details, and store elements that entertain customers.

By exploring, and ultimately deeply understanding, a brand's emotional relevance to its target customer through the Head, Heart, Gut framework, Desgrippes Gobé reveals how a company can realize its brand vision through its various marketing communications.

2. Brand Management System (BMS)

"What relationship and what intimacy will my brand create with its audience, and what role will each of my signs and media play? Today, this is one of the major questions in branding." —François Caratgé, General Manager, Desgrippes Gobé Paris

The Brand Management System created by Desgrippes Gobé is a tool for assessing the many facets of a brand's visual personality and its efficiency in the marketplace. Because a brand's identity expression must reach its customer where and when he or she wants to be reached, BMS presents a strategy for accompanying or escorting a consumer through his or her daily activities.

Desgrippes Gobé first measures the levels of a consumer's receptivity to a brand's personality in the course of his daily life—a receptivity that changes depending on whether he is commuting to work, at a nightclub or a ballgame, or on vacation. The team determines when a customer wants to be impacted by the brand presence and when he wants to be contacted. Impact is important when a brand needs to get practical or directional information across; here the emotional relevance is low and the rational, "head" expectations of the customer are addressed. Contact is about the human touch, those instances when the customer wants to get a feel for the brand and interact with it in a personal way. Contact takes place through the atmosphere of a store environment, the community feel the brand presence inspires, and its ability to interact online or on the street.

The Brand Management System ensures that a brand's message matches people's acceptance levels and expectations through a multidimensional, sensitive brand dialogue. By understanding these different moments in

time and tailoring brand presence programs to interact with consumers with sensitivity and innovation, memorable, emotionally relevant contact with consumers can be attained. A brand becomes like a friend, interacting with the consumer in a sympathetic way.

3. SENSE®

"Emotional branding is a means of creating a personal dialogue with consumers. Consumers today expect their brands to know them intimately and individually, with a solid understanding of their needs and cultural orientation." —Marc Gobé

The design process begins with SENSE®, which combines observation and creativity with disciplined research techniques to ensure that design ideas are grounded in the real-life experiences of the target audience. SENSE® s a visual process that identifies a product's equities, profiles the customer, analyzes the competition, and develops a multidimensional, emotionally charged visual and sensual vocabulary.

SENSE® begins with an analysis of the brand's inherent values and looks closely at the many ways it interacts with the consumer—intellectually, visually, associatively, and sensorially. The customer profile is carefully illustrated to define the role the product plays within his or her lifestyle. Working with this profile, the design team finalizes a rich

palette of imagery that will bring the customer's emotional connection with the brand to life.

With this image-based strategy in place, the team then moves into a full-scale creative exploration in four different design disciplines: graphic design, industrial design, architecture, and interactive design. The result is powerful, initiating coordinated packaging, graphics, retail environments, and interactive design platforms that are strategically appropriate and that generate an emotional response in the customer to give the company a more competitive edge.

Case Studies

Foreword

Anne Hellman

Upon first meeting the Desgrippes Gobé group, I was a relative newcomer to the branding world. Now I must say my eyes have been opened. Not only did this remarkable agency open its archives to me, but it also taught me what I am sure amounts to an elevated crash course in brand design. What a world—and one that only grows wider every day.

A large part of collecting material for this book was gathering the immensely creative insights of the Desgrippes Gobé designers themselves. Each designer has his or her particular take and style to contribute to the overall effort of Desgrippes Gobé Worldwide, and each generously shared with me a unique articulation of the emotional brand experience. Through email and telephone conversations, I received invaluable suggestions and visions on each project from points around the globe, including Paris, Hong Kong, Seoul, Brussels, and Tokyo. It quickly became apparent how connected this group really is, despite its international spread.

I would especially like to thank the following designers, project managers, and others who contributed quotes, images, material, and helpful advice on the different case studies in this book; from Asia-Pacific: Craig Briggs, Juan Castilla, Missla Libsekal, Seung Mok Kim, and Yoko Iwasaki; from Europe: Nadège des Closets, Françoise Chevalier, Jean Jacques and Brigitte Evrard, Sophie Liebermann, François Caratgé, Alain Doré, and Elie Hasbani; and from New York City: Valérie Le Deroff, Dana Gerhards, Hannah Yampolsky, Peter Levine, Sam O'Donahue, Federico Chieli, John Schroeder, Lenny Stein, and especially Jacquelyn Wosilius.

AIR FRANCE

When Air France first contacted Desgrippes Gobé, the company wanted to affirm its position as one of the top airlines in the world. Desgrippes Gobé's task was to spark a new corporate image for the brand based on its core values of French elegance and assurance, giving it renewed momentum, vision, and imagination. A mythic brand rich in associations with the glamorous life—as celebrities including Brigitte Bardot, Audrey Hepburn, and Marilyn Monroe once posed for photographs on the company's boarding ramps—Air France has always conveyed an aura of French sophistication—of luxury *à la française*. In building the new visual presence, Desgrippes Gobé updated and strengthened the brand's attributes of French refinement and glamour.

Ambition, Vision, Differentiation

Mounting pressures caused by consolidation in the industry and increased competition among carriers for business and leisure travelers made it imperative that Air France reestablish its presence as a leading airline. "In a context of banality and predictability in the world of air travel, it became a real necessity for Air France to give a strong and differentiating promise to travelers," assert François Caratgé, general manager, and Alain Doré, creative director, both brand managers for Air France. "Our role as a dedicated design agency was to give life to the ambition of the brand, which was to 'make the sky the most beautiful place on earth.'" To accomplish this, Desgrippes Gobé's objective was to make Air France the most beautiful airline in the world.

As a purely French company, the airline embodies many contrasts, a mix of styles, and even contradictions, between history and innovation, classical creation and modern design. This is representative of the country itself, where the very old meets the very new, as with I. M. Pei's pyramid at the Musée du Louvre, integrating extreme modernity into a celebrated monument of cultural history. Air France wanted to embrace this concept of itself as an established, heritage brand that was also young and vibrant, modern and future-oriented. It is this mix of contrasts that forms the soul of the Air France brand.

The first-class lounge in the Air France terminal unites a number of pared-down yet stylish decorative elements. Subdued lighting, pale wood walls, and leather armchairs and couches supply just the right amount of comfort.

"In a context of banality and predictability in the world of air travel, it became a real necessity for Air France to give a strong and differentiating promise to travelers. Our role as a dedicated design agency was to give life to the ambition of the brand, which was to 'make the sky the most beautiful place on earth.'"
—François Caratgé, General Manager, and Alain Doré, Creative Director, Desgrippes Gobé Paris, Brand Managers for Air France

From the beginning, Air France differentiated itself from other airlines by making different choices: it chose to keep the first-class cabin when competitors were discontinuing it; it moved to embellish the art of traveling by improving and enhancing aesthetics when other airlines were moving toward standardization.

Three, Two, One . . . Contact

The first step of the brand's rebirth was to analyze the range of consumer segments the airline reached, its contact points with consumers, and its emotional frame of reference. The role of each of Air France's communications was redefined with respect to consumer expectations. Depending on where the traveler is during their experience with the brand, their needs vary: some of them are purely rational concerns, such as credibility, safety, and security (for example, in the boarding process). In other situations, the traveler is receptive to the more imaginative messages of pleasure, community, and the fantasy of travel.

Desgrippes Gobé's role was to set the scene for the interaction between the imaginary and the real and to find ways to express vocabularies that could be adapted to fit each situation. The corporate identity is needed most when the brand must help and guide the traveler, so Desgrippes Gobé designed the Air France identity to make a strong impression on the minds of travelers. In contrast, the brand's imaginary communications invite the traveler to daydream. They are subtler than a simple logo; they create a vocabulary that conveys the brand's emotional value and ultimately allows travelers to customize their individual travel experiences.

"When the traveler is particularly receptive, the message can be emotive and can call upon their imagination, whereas when their receptivity is low, the message has to be understood instantaneously," explain François Caratgé and Alain Doré. "The objective is to create brand reflexes, to go deeper into the reference points that are associated with the brand. Air France wanted to create a deep and personalized link with travelers, so that it is no longer chosen arbitrarily but because it is the preferred one."

Desgrippes Gobé performed a brand experience audit, classifying each point of contact to determine how the airline was communicating with its target audiences and to envision the optimal way of doing so. What type of expectations and receptivity did the traveler have in the interior of the sales office? What about the plane interior? Did it effectively meet customers' expectations? The audit revealed that while Air France's identity system was appropriate in some applications, it was missing crucial opportunities in others.

First-class Air France customers with time before or between flights can sit back and read a book or work on their laptops in the airy new lounge. The spacious room combines warm wood tones, modern yet comfortable leather furniture in shades of deep blue and tan, and elegant hints of the airline's blue-white-and-red theme to create a space that is welcoming and relaxing, equally conducive to hanging out as it is to getting work done. Glass-panel walls separating different areas allow light from the standing lamps as well as natural light from the windows to penetrate throughout.

Even the restrooms in the Air France terminal have been redecorated to convey a sense of clean modernity and light. Chrome surfaces reflect the stylish white lighting and extend the themes of high technology and sophistication of the overall visual identity system.

With views to the outdoors, the first-class lounge provides a welcoming and relaxing place to wait for a flight. Glossy chrome standing lamps provide a warm, subdued glow that reflects evenly off the pale wood walls. The lounge combines comfort with pristine airiness, juxtaposing sleek, ergonomic chairs with simply designed tables.

For example, by the time a traveler steps onboard an Air France airplane, they have come to the Air France terminal, checked in at the Air France counter, passed through the Air France gate, and have received an Air France boarding pass from an Air France steward. Once on the plane, the primary message needn't be simply that the plane belongs to Air France: here was an opportunity to impact the traveler in a different way. Desgrippes Gobé's audit concluded that the interior of the plane offered a chance to communicate with the customer on a more sensory level.

The Design Solution

Air France commissioned Desgrippes Gobé to create an all-encompassing program for the airline's brand presence, from the plane interiors to customer lounges to flight menus, brochures, and the company Web site. Culling the research from the brand audit, Desgrippes Gobé created a visual territory, or system of visual elements, for each of the emotional levels. The visual system it developed for the more rational "identity" communications—the exterior of the sales offices and boarding gates—focuses on the attributes of credibility, modern technology, international reach, and French elegance, and includes any communication in which the identification of the Air France brand is of primary importance, such as signage, timetables, and enrollment forms. Here Desgrippes Gobé centers the visuals around core identity items—the strong, aerodynamic logo and red, white, and blue color palette along with colorful, dynamic stripes to create a sense of safety as well as speed.

Then comes the "imaginary" communications—all the interactive applications, such as the sales office interiors, passenger lounges, and the Air France Web site. Here Desgrippes Gobé emphasizes community, personalized service, and practical comfort. The new visual system introduces a warmer color palette and materials. Passenger lounges incorporate warm wood tones and natural fabrics to give the space a clean and comfortable feel.

Plane interiors, direct mail, menu cards, and advertising tap directly into the positive emotional territory of travel over transportation. The plush first-class reclining lounges and the crisp, designs of the business- and coach-class cabins accentuate feelings of pleasure, "sweet dreams," and escape. The visual system introduces a broader, softer color palette and a stronger use of imagery and is recommended for all applications in which the primary goal is brand communication, not identification.

Taking the Results Sky-High

A project such as Air France encompasses much more than the creation of graphic elements: it consists of building a deep and lasting vision of and for the brand. Desgrippes Gobé made ambition, vision, and differentiation the three main components of its branding strategy and managed every message to ensure that it contributed to the brand image in the most efficient and consistent way. Today, Desgrippes Gobé guides Air France in their present brand program as well as in their vision for the brand three to four years ahead. The firm has devised a platform for the continued development of applications and the updating of imagery to keep it in line with the brand strategy as it evolves. In its ongoing relationship with Air France, Desgrippes Gobé continues to define key trends and create a real vision of what Air France can be in the future.

Above top: The Air France website poses the strong, aerodynamic logo against a serene sky background, foregrounding Air France's signature colors of blue, white, and red. The image plays on the airline's affirmed role as international connoisseur that also has a sense of fun and adventure. Incorporating modern, sans-serif letter-forms and playful imagery, the design upholds key identity attributes of credibility, modern technology, international reach, and French elegance as well as the more sensitive, imaginary elements of travel.
Above bottom: The first-class cabins feature reclinable leather seats that extend into a full-length bed, complete with reading lamp and bedside table. Elements of polished warm wood, crisp white sheets, and hints of Air France red provide a cozy, luxurious place to settle down for an overnight flight.

WINTER OLYMPIC GAMES

ALBERTVILLE, FRANCE, 1992

The commission to design a visual identity for the 1992 Albertville Winter Olympics was unique in the history of the brand. Breaking from tradition, the Albertville Olympic Games committee decided to implement a unifying image for the Games that could be adapted to a variety of venues and establish a consistent graphic identity for the event. Until then, the Olympic city's image had never been retained as the basis for an overall identity system, but in this case the Albertville committee was willing to expand upon it.

Through the strong commitment of Jean-Claude Killy and Michel Barnier, co-presidents of the committee, an unprecedented rupture with convention ignited the design from the get-go. Deeply involved with the event's communications, Killy and Barnier stood behind the new vision proposed by Desgrippes Gobé. Their enthusiasm incited a turn away from traditional ways of thinking about the Games toward a more emotional, more sensitive vision, while preserving the official scope integral to this type of world event.

Desgrippes Gobé's objective was to create more than a logo, but a comprehensive territory of signs and expressions to communicate the event in its entirety. The Albertville Olympic Games consisted of thirteen different ski resorts, each with its own unique personality and competitive edge. The design team aimed to awaken a cohesive spirit within the Games, one that was about universality, sportsmanship, and fair competition.

What an Image Can Do

The role of the founding image was crucial to this objective. Every element of the design was created to strengthen the coherence of the identity system, from the directionals and pictograms to uniforms and any graphic that appeared on the Olympic courses.

Desgrippes Gobé presented the initial proposal in the form of an exhibition at the mythic Comédie Française in Paris four years before the Albertville Games. The presentation was conducted like a circus, with thirteen different panels, or "rings," which were revealed one after the other to demonstrate the powerful link between each consecutive element. Once all of the panels had been unveiled, those in attendance felt completely immersed in what the Games would look like four years later. The presentation helped to inspire a powerful emotional reaction in the audience, bonding them to the event. The designs relied on gestural drawings that communicated the speed and free-spiritedness of the competitions, as well as their dynamic alpine setting.

"From the beginning, the creation was strong, coherent. Every design element was thought through at the same time," recalls creative director Alain Doré.

Olympic Design

Killy and Barnier supported the new graphics proposed by Desgrippes Gobé, helping to introduce innovative, emotional, and sensitive communications into the Albertville Games and into the Olympic Games platform moving forward. Each graphic component conveys the spirit of the Games, a spirit that is universal and immediately palpable to audiences around the world. The Olympics are a time-honored event that people everywhere grow up with, and this commonality is crucial not only to the games themselves, but also to how those games are portrayed in all of their aspects.

The graphic codes that Desgrippes Gobé created balance a series of opposites, heightening the friction and excitement within the design. The codes navigate between a sense of sportive discipline and one of celebration, between a structured tradition and a strong spontaneity, between the authoritative strictness of the Olympic organization and a world of fantasy where wishes really do come true.

Desgrippes Gobé's goal was to make the Olympic Games as open and approachable as possible. The team created an abundance of imagery, reflecting the breadth of the world-renowned event while also preserving its basic ethics. "We put four complete years of work, passion, and commitment into sixteen days of games," says Doré. "The investment was huge, and the result was a resounding success."

In total, three hundred people worked on the project, from sponsors to the teams themselves, with the intention of creating an event that could truly be shared by the worldwide community. The imagery invites all ages to participate in the Games, making them festive and easy to understand.

The mascot of the Albertville Winter Olympic Games is an elf-like star figure with a red cap rendered in a lively hand-drawn style. The slogan "world youthfulness" invites Olympics enthusiasts of all ages to participate and makes the event something that is festive and approachable as well as competitive.

JEUNESSE DU MONDE

SAVOIE 1992 · FRANCE

"We put four complete years of work, passion, and commitment into sixteen days of games. The investment was huge, and the result was a resounding success."

—Alain Doré, Creative Director, Desgrippes Gobé Paris

The graphics rely on gestural drawings in the Olympic primary colors to communicate speed and free-spiritedness.

A poster for the Olympic Flame Route.

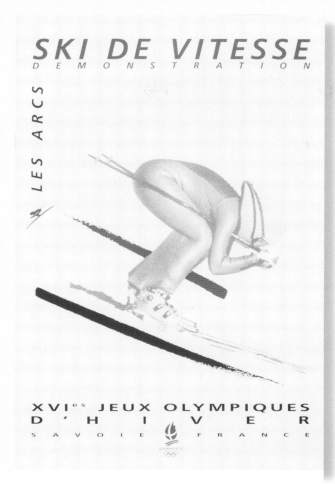

A poster for the alpine skiing event balances a sense of sportive discipline and speed with spontaneous brushstrokes of color.

Signage on site at the Albertville Games combines gestural swatches of color with a strong sans-serif typeface for easy readability.

Brochures for the Albertville Games.

AMÉLIE

Conveniently, Seoul's Ewha University students can experience Europe without wandering too far from campus. Amélie, a clean modern tea salon and bakery, is the latest concept from the innovative Korean Paris-Croissant group, for which Desgrippes Gobé designed Paris-Baguette, a takeaway bakery concept that has been applied to more than twelve hundred sales sites throughout Korea. For the Amélie project, Desgrippes Gobé took on every step of the branding process, from creating the brand name to the architectural design of the shop to the visual identity, including logo, packaging, server uniforms, lighting, flooring, furniture, fixtures, and tableware.

Blending the Old with the New

Amélie owes its unique ambience to the untraditional materials the design team used to build the space and convey its bright, fresh vibe. The classic wallpaper prints created with the new Amélie pattern and synthetic wood-grain flooring remind visitors of a classic past, albeit a classicism infused with the definitively contemporary. Likewise, the modern color palette cleverly imitates the foods on display in the luminous glass cases.

"Stepping into an Amélie shop, customers take a journey through time that combines past and future, tradition and modernity," explains Joël Desgrippes. "The new 'cake-shop' concept creates its own sociable world and invites visitors to discover gourmet pleasures by extending the sensation of the delicious foods it offers into the overall architectural concept of the store itself."

Desgrippes Gobé sought a simple and classic French first name to give the bakery its unmistakable Euro-French accent. The name also needed to be four syllables or less and easy to pronounce in Hangul, the Korean language. The very Parisian "Amélie" was the perfect solution. The illuminated-manuscript style of the "A" in the logo reinforces the brand's European and particularly French origins, while decorative details add to the quirky atmosphere of the shop interior: French-style

The Amélie logo and monogram combine the aesthetics of French illuminated manuscripts with a modern typeface and contemporary color combination. The sans-serif type of the brand name stands out against the appetizing hues of brown, pale blue, and lemon yellow, which give the logo its playful, "edible" feel.

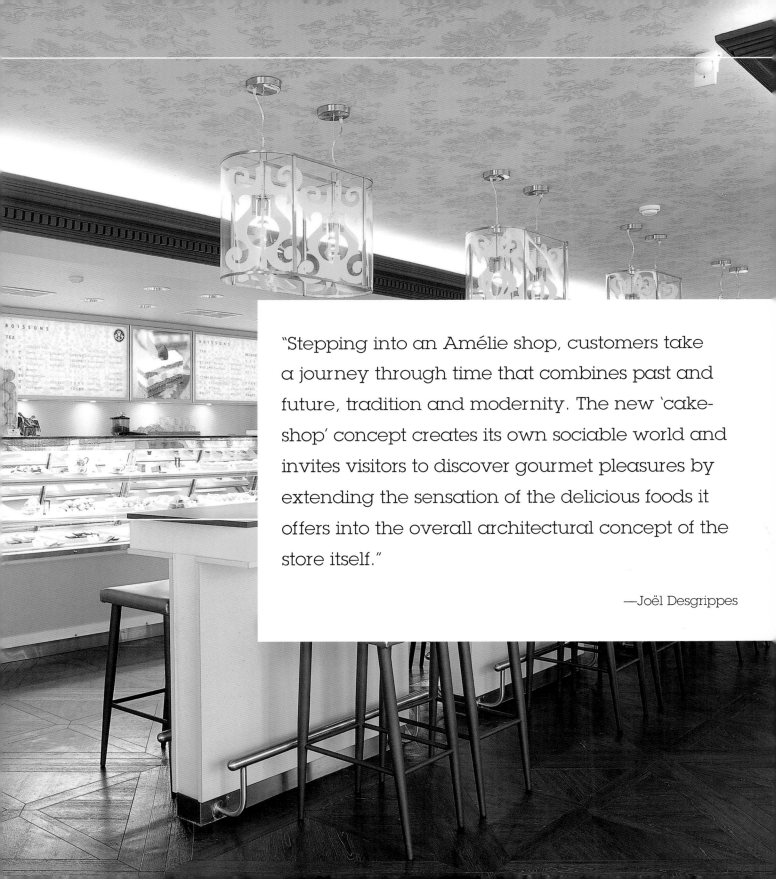

"Stepping into an Amélie shop, customers take a journey through time that combines past and future, tradition and modernity. The new 'cake-shop' concept creates its own sociable world and invites visitors to discover gourmet pleasures by extending the sensation of the delicious foods it offers into the overall architectural concept of the store itself."

—Joël Desgrippes

floors, wallpaper created specially in France and inspired by eighteenth-century flower patterns, beaded curtains hanging from the ceiling to structure the space and make it friendly, and a molded resin cornice reminiscent of traditional French designs. But the design team did not focus solely on the French theme: a detail in the tables allowing for handbags to be placed close by demonstrates their intimate understanding of the customer—today's young Korean woman.

Gourmet Color

Interplaying seemingly incongruous colors and materials to highlight gourmet flavors and pleasures was Desgrippes Gobé's special tactic for the project. The team selected only cheery, mouth-watering colors, such as "anis vanilla," "sugar blue," and "salty caramel," to create an eatery that is undeniably young and chic though still genuinely gourmand. The armchairs are made with a pearly plastic that blends with the shimmering white walls, while the rich chocolate-brown of the logo echoed in the cornice warms the room. Every element contributes to the enjoyment of similarly colored pastries.

Amélie is a concept that not only awakens the senses and taste buds but also takes its customers (who are bound to return again and again) on a real-life voyage that is both sensorial and cultural.

The menu welcomes customers to the tea lounge with buoyant, stylish colors and patterns, while crisp white leather chairs and recessed lighting create an atmosphere conducive to casual mingling. Separate eating areas are delineated by white beaded curtains, which add an element of youthfulness as well as a sense of both structure and flow.

The Amélie shop glows with warmth and sociability even at night.

The Amélie packaging incorporates the pale luminescent coloring of the visual system in creative combinations.

Above: The restroom features a sink shaped like a fondant-frosted layer cake, stylish chrome faucet, and hints of the floral wallpaper and lampshade pattern found in the main room.

Below: The display cases combine tradition with modernity, featuring glowing glass panes that show off Amélie's delicious offerings. The case's stylish chrome edges and illuminated paneling in the shop's unconventional yellow further unite the overall aesthetic.

The interior of the bakery radiates shades of white, lemon yellow, and pale blue, giving the room a sunny, clean air. Chrome stools and accents throughout give it its utterly contemporary feel, while the floral wallpaper design, lampshades, and ornate ceiling cornice remind the visitor that they are stepping into a gourmet world of tradition as well as fashion.

Even the uniforms were designed to coincide with the visual elements of the shop interior.

ANN TAYLOR

By the early nineties, Ann Taylor had established a retail identity that was at risk of losing the interest of a new generation of young women. At the same time, because of the rising number of these young women entering the workforce and creating careers as well as leisure lifestyles for themselves, Ann Taylor was uniquely positioned to take advantage of the changing times. Always a practical-minded woman, the new desired Ann Taylor customer was active both socially and in the working world. A revamped identity for the brand would have to flesh out the pre-nineties go-to-work look to encompass the fullness and vibrancy of a woman's life, including the personal care products she uses; her evening, weekend, and special occasion apparel, and the fragrances she favors. The possibilities were endless.

Becoming Ann Taylor

In 1992, Ann Taylor's challenge was to overturn a decline in sales and apparel offerings that had resulted in diminished customer loyalty. Desgrippes Gobé approached the case by homing in on the personality behind the Ann Taylor identity. The first step was to use the SENSE® program to create a story for the brand that personalized the fictitious "Ann." Through conducting SENSE®, the Desgrippes Gobé team identifies a product's equities, profiles the customer, analyzes the competition, and develops a multidimensional, emotionally charged visual and sensual vocabulary that then serves as the foundation for the design process. The team collaborated with the company's top twelve managers and buyers and a trusted editor to determine the values embraced by the Ann Taylor customer, which were defined as authenticity, balance, independence, and friendship. This exercise helped the team build the persona of Ann Taylor—an independent, truthful, elegant, and approachable woman—and infused the company as a whole with new spirit and passion. "Often, managers would review products in the new collection and comment, 'Ann would never do this', or, 'This is very consistent with her voice'," muses Gobé.

Using these values as the basis for the new brand identity, the design objective was to develop packaging and retail environments that felt honest, natural, and personal, reflecting the individuality of the brand—and, by extension, its customers—in all of the brand's manifestations, from its product line to flagship stores in New York and San Francisco.

The spacious foyer greets customers with accents of light wood and fresh flowers, as though they have just stepped into Ann Taylor's gracious home. An elegant curved stairway leads away from the foyer.

"Often, managers would review products in the new collection and comment, 'Ann would never do this', or, 'This is very consistent with her voice.'"

—Marc Gobé

The skylight on the top floor illuminates the clean, crisp store spaces, wood floors, and unique accents such as custom fixtures and sculpted-wood hand railing for the staircase.

Above left: The Ann Taylor flagship store on Madison Avenue in New York was designed to look and feel like Ann's uptown residence. Inspired by townhouses in the neighborhood, the limestone façade invites you into the multilevel, 40,000-square-foot space with luminous sidewalk windows and an entryway reminiscent of an upscale city residence.

Above left: Constructed of limestone and glass, the staircase spirals up through all five levels of the store under an expansive skylight, providing a visually stunning centerpiece for the space. **Above right:** The façade of an Ann Taylor Loft outlet store beckons younger Ann Taylor customers in, displaying a more relaxed and open atttiude while still retaining its link to the "mother" store.

"The Ann Taylor woman is real, unpretentious, and practical-minded," Gobé emphasizes. "To reflect her tastes, the store design is elegant, sophisticated, refined and, through its full range of merchandise, suits her needs for total wardrobing." Ann Taylor would be viewed as a trusted friend who shares the same values and aspirations as its customers, and who understands their needs and concerns.

In keeping with the new identity, the design team created product packaging and shopping bags from recycled materials in natural-colored papers and textures to convey a sense of ease and authenticity. The brand's ink-blue corporate color was reintroduced, this time in a sleek Bodoni typeface updated with the handwritten tag line "Destination" to reference this new, young woman's purposeful determination—she was going places. New box shapes, navy grosgrain ribbons, and shopping bags with a photograph of a multifaceted and real-looking woman were added to give character and personality to the total image.

More than just revitalizing and enhancing Ann Taylor's elegant fashion signature, the new identity initiated a fully realized brand program, one that included a reconceived store architecture and atmosphere, as well as exciting new merchandise. The launch of the new image in March 1993 recaptured the essence of Ann Taylor's personality in the nineties, providing it with a platform from which to evolve with the times. Desgrippes Gobé's efforts were awarded the 1994 International Brand Packaging Gold Medal for Corporate Identity, and Ann Taylor became one of the premiere moderate-priced clothing brands for professional women in America.

Flagship Atmosphere Coast to Coast

Walking into the Ann Taylor store on Madison Avenue, the Desgrippes Gobé team conceptualized that it would be like walking into the home of Ann Taylor herself, a woman who knows how to host, how to compose a welcoming atmosphere, and most important, how to live. "Retail designers have the opportunity to impact society by bringing a renewed sense of beauty to all channels of distribution," says Gobé. "People are looking for experiences of newness and excitement within stores. Furthermore, retail environments should be inspired by the products they sell in a way that brings total consistency to the brand image."

To create the 40,000-square-foot flagship store, Desgrippes Gobé's design strategy spiraled out from the personality it had conceived for the brand starting in 1992: the practical-minded yet adventurous and independent woman who lived in an elegant yet natural interior. From the townhouse-inspired façade clad in limestone to the spacious foyer accented with light wood tones and fresh flowers, customers immediately feel as though they are stepping into an upscale version of the Ann Taylor retail identity. This is her uptown residence, the store says; this is where she lives and entertains, and it is also a strong force in the creation of her tastes. The store spaces are clean and crisp, refined and enriched with warm, tactile materials. Custom fixtures in glass and wood with nickel accents outline displays of clothing, perfume, and accessories.

The centerpiece of the plan is an elegantly curved staircase made of limestone and glass, which spirals up through five floors of merchandise to arrive at a glowing skylight. On

The entrance and foyer of the Ann Taylor flagship store in San Francisco echoes the New York store with an upscale entryway and warm and welcoming interior. The wood floors, fresh flowers, and curved stairway are recognizable Ann Taylor elements that evoke the feeling of entering an elegant home.

the second floor, double-height windows draw in natural light, diffusing it throughout the upper levels. An exclusive personal shopping area, or "comfort zone," is equipped with a built-in desk, including a spot to plug in your laptop. These personalized touches are all part of Ann Taylor's commitment to service as well as a reflection of the multiple roles the target customer fulfills in her daily life. An intimate mezzanine area is exclusively devoted to the "Destination" product line, presenting a refined and stimulating array of fragrances, bath and body products, and scented items for the home.

Desgrippes Gobé lightened the atmosphere of the retail interior by using natural, monochromatic colors that communicate the unpretentious side of the Ann Taylor customer, accented by the brand's signature navy blue. The furnishings are rendered in sensuous shapes in a mix of warm and cool materials such as bronze, stone, frosted green glass, and auburn wood, which give textural contrast to the space. Sculpted details on fixtures, door handles, and railings add a human, homelike touch to personalize the store design.

A flagship store in San Francisco soon followed in the footsteps of the New York store, extending the revitalized Ann Taylor aesthetic, even the "woman" herself, to both coasts. The Ann Taylor brand presence could be felt by all women everywhere, whether starting a first job or moving into the heights of a full career at the office and in the home. By creating an atmosphere that was upscale and relaxed at the same time, Ann Taylor could make a full range of different women feel "at home" in its stores. Both the New York and San Francisco stores won top retail design merits in 1996 and 1997.

Below left: The Destination line includes a wide array of refined, all-natural bath, body, and home products in line with the Ann Taylor customer's values of authenticity, naturalness, simplicity, and humor. **Below right:** Like the New York flagship store, the San Francisco retail environment combines elements of the home—a stylish rug, wood table, and a potted orchid—with unfussy clothing displays. Natural touches such as wood panels and glass shelving provide the perfect complement to the sophisticated simplicity of the clothing designs.

Top images and center right: Elements of the Ann Taylor retail identity such as shopping bags and product packaging play a key role in extending the brand's personality outside the store. Shopping bags were made of natural, or off-white paper, and lettering was kept simple in Ann Taylor navy to reinforce the values of the target customer. One shopping bag pictures a practical, youthful woman to validate the store's bond with its customers. **Center left:** Bottle designs for the Destination fragrance and body products are sheer and feminine, communicating purity as well as sensuality. Color and material choices such as gunmetal and frosted glass for the flacon, and wood and textured paper for the box, reinforce the brand's core palette.

The Places You'll Go

The expanded Destination line included not only a woman's total wardrobe needs but also an array of refined, all-natural bath, body, and home products. The challenge for the packaging design was to achieve a perfect accord with its inspiration: the Ann Taylor customer and her values of authenticity, naturalness, and simplicity as well as sensuality, adventure, and humor. Desgrippes Gobé's strategy was to encapsulate the equities of the new brand image and, by extension, the aesthetics and values of the customer. The Destination fragrance is a clean, refreshing, and personal scent. With sheer packaging and a delicate touch of femininity, Destination products communicate a purity that permeates the store environment itself.

The bottle and box designs for the product line express its fresh, natural, and sensual attributes. Color and material choices such as gunmetal and frosted glass for the bottle, and wood and textured paper for the box, reinforce the brand's core palette. The nature-based shapes encourage shoppers to interact with the containers, integral to any fragrance's package design. The ease and authenticity consistent with the experience of shopping at an Ann Taylor store are reiterated in the look and feel of the box, and the liquid's cool blue cast adds an uplifting air. The Destination packaging design won the PDC Gold Award in 1996, among many other distinctions.

The open-air plan and concrete floors of the Ann Taylor Loft outlet store suggest a warehouse converted into a residence while fulfilling the brand's commercial purposes. Natural wood, canvas, ink-blue, and brushed-nickel elements link back to the main store concept, while helping the space feel industrial at the same time.

Loft Life

The Ann Taylor Loft concept was a savvy outgrowth of the revitalized brand presence, which was more about lifestyle and total life experience as well as the home. Ann Taylor's Loft stores spoke to the younger, hipper generation of shoppers who have crafted alternative living spaces and likewise crave an alternative, more casual look. These days, you can't walk down a New York City sidewalk without seeing a woman on her way to work toting a Loft shopping bag, used that weekend to hold her new purchases and now reconceived as a carrier for lunch or gym shoes. Loft accentuated the new Ann Taylor identity and brought it home to the youth generation.

Desgrippes Gobé helped name and conceive this new concept "loft" after Ann's daughter's lifestyle. The Loft outlet store encompasses its own branded identity and distinct merchandise, while preserving its link to the "mother" store. The outlet retail environment offered an opportunity to capitalize on the loft concept. By selecting as its point of inspiration an open loft space much like that which a young woman might inhabit early in her career, the design team created an interior with a simple, unpretentious, downtown feel, one that captures the relaxed, late-nineties attitude.

Simple, functional fixture designs and an open-air plan suggest a warehouse converted into a residence that also fulfills its commercial purpose. Loft honors Ann Taylor's natural wood, canvas, ink-blue, and brushed-nickel palette while introducing new features such as a media center that communicate a residential comfort and a sensitivity to the lifestyle of the target customer. Exposed trusswork and whitewashed brick walls lighten the vast horizontality of the space, while skylights and a window façade bring natural light into the store. The clothing racks emphasize the ceiling height—a hallmark of loft spaces—but also facilitate circulation by allowing shoppers to access garments from both sides. Flexible wood and nickel shelving units that show an appreciation for honest design run along the perimeter and define separate areas within the store while also accommodating evolving display needs based on seasons or collections. Mirrors and ladders on wheels allow for quick access to stock and reinforce the values of ease and practicality. Concrete floors complete the renovated aesthetic.

Designs for both the Loft and the Ann Taylor flagship incorporated seating and entertainment areas for men and children. Books, magazines, toys, and a wide-screen television keep Dad and the kids busy while wives and mothers can enjoy a little "me time."

The design won Graphis' Design and Packaging Annuals in 1997, as well as many other awards worldwide.

AOL

Reinventing the AOL visual identity could have been a risky undertaking. Here was the company known for first getting America onto the Internet, and many of the more than 22 million subscribers were those who had started out with AOL back in the day. A new company logo could possibly alienate those users who were not computer-savvy enough to keep up with the change. But after conducting widespread research—more than 10,000 consumers were surveyed—AOL management and the Desgrippes Gobé team realized that consumers had a love-hate relationship with the brand and that a revamped logo would help rejecters disassociate the brand from its bygone and outdated persona. Likewise, research showed that a new logo would champion the support of those who loved the brand, because those users already had expectations that online brands should be constantly updated and improved.

The AOL Challenge

AOL management wanted to signal that the brand was changing. Though it was viewed as a pioneer and retained a huge brand awareness, in 2003 the AOL brand had become perceived as too simplistic and linked to dial-up connectivity, as opposed to new high-speed broadband or cable connections. The AOL image was proving to be serious baggage as the market shifted to high-speed connectivity, which offered richer online experiences for consumers, and these brand perceptions were prohibiting AOL from capturing high-speed market share. The AOL identity needed to communicate that AOL was relevant to people's lives, that it was more than just a dial-up connection.

The visual identities of media and Internet companies today must be iconic and memorable because they appear on so many different applications—on the Web, on TV, in print. AOL was up against younger Internet portals that brandished vibrant, dynamic logos. Its main competitors were Yahoo! and MSN, which offered similar content and products (such as Mail and Instant Messenger). Google was also quickly becoming a competitor with its search and mail products. But as AOL was developing more of its own programming and content, it would soon be competing with media networks and cable channels such as MTV, Nickelodeon, and NBC. The brand's visual identity would need to reflect its advanced capabilities and positioning with respect to its competitors.

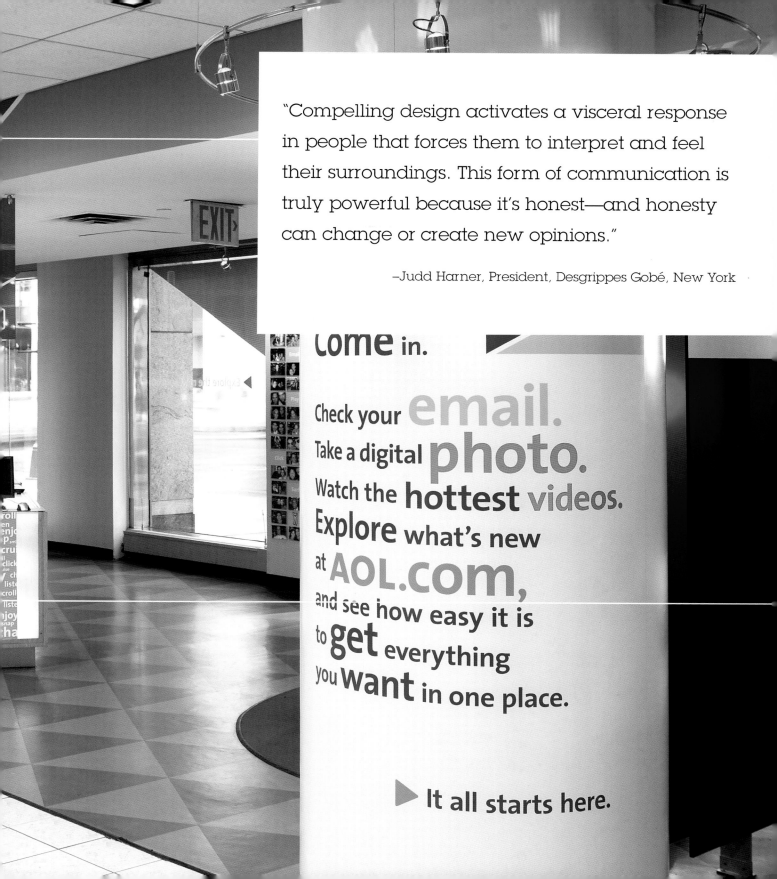

"Compelling design activates a visceral response in people that forces them to interpret and feel their surroundings. This form of communication is truly powerful because it's honest—and honesty can change or create new opinions."

–Judd Harner, President, Desgrippes Gobé, New York

COME in.

Check your **email.**

Take a digital **photo.**

Watch the **hottest** videos.

Explore what's new

at **AOL.COM,**

and see how easy it is

to **get** everything

you **want** in one place.

▶ It all starts here.

The original AOL logo (left) capitalized on the power stance of the triangle shape. For the new logo (right), Desgrippes Gobé discovered that the triangle could be tilted to become an arrow pointing into the future.

A New Brand Positioning

AOL's most powerful attribute was a tremendous emotional connection with customers. And it's precisely this type of connection that Desgrippes Gobé specializes in and works to reinforce. "The new identity would have to connect with people in a different way, bringing a message of change, innovation, and leadership," says Marc Gobé. "We needed to shift the old identity from that of a comforting friend who makes using the Internet easy to the position of being a savvy, trusted partner. We needed to show that AOL offers products and services that are innovative and smart, but it also offers security and protection for families. Most importantly, we had to show its commitment to society."

Desgrippes Gobé first conducted Brand Focus with the AOL team to home in on visuals that would help clarify its vision and define the new brand positioning. The visuals selected expressed intuitive and effortless discoveries, colors that were bold and fun, a spirit of independence, and a sense of security. The future of the brand in the team's mind was a bright and imaginative one. Positive attributes such as "connected", "social", "friendly", "comfortable", and "helpful" were targeted for strengthening into desired attributes such as "approachable", "responsive", "effortless", and "dynamic". Potentially negative and negative attributes such as the fact that AOL was so big, and descriptives such as "arrogant",

"relentless", and "training wheels" were pinpointed for conversion into "powerful advocate", "trustworthy", and "innovative leader".

On top of the insight gathered through Brand Focus, the Desgrippes Gobé team also surveyed AOL members to find out what they loved, what they hated, and most importantly, what they were missing in the AOL brand. Consumers said that what they missed most was the excitement they felt when they first joined AOL. They wanted AOL to inspire them the way it did when they first got online. They wanted to feel that AOL understood their needs and worked with them, for them, and not against them. They wanted AOL to catch up to their sophisticated use of the Internet and take a leadership position once again. Just as it had as a young brand, consumers wanted AOL to guide them to what was new and unexpected.

A New Logo

The logo had to signify a fresh start and announce that, like all other cutting-edge technology businesses, AOL too was constantly updating and improving its services and looking to the future. The original AOL triangle mark had value as a recognizable shape, but on the whole it had faded into the cyberspace background. Desgrippes Gobé wanted to

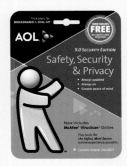

AOL's new packaging graphics (far left) are cleaner and more contemporary and communicate a higher-quality product. The graphics incorporate the friendlier logo and figure as well as a hint of the mosaic pattern used throughout the new visual identity in vibrant simplified colors. Older packagings were busy and overly crammed with imagery, conveying a lower-quality aesthetic.

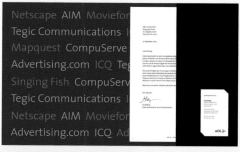
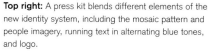

Top right: A press kit blends different elements of the new identity system, including the mosaic pattern and people imagery, running text in alternating blue tones, and logo.
Top left and bottom right: Elements of the business system, including brochures, stationery, and business cards, were designed to uphold the new AOL aesthetic. An embossed folder to be used internally carries the visual system into all corners of the corporate identity.

transform it into something new, something that would stand out. With a slight tilt, they discovered that the triangle could be turned into an arrow pointing forward into the future.

"We did not have to keep the triangle, but the shape had tremendous awareness among consumers," explains Gobé. Current and past AOL members consistently recalled two elements of the first logo as being key to what AOL stands for: the color blue and the triangle. Redesigning it as an arrow changed the logo from a marker to a message. The arrow proclaimed the company's commitment to guiding users to new experiences and continually providing new features and services, while preserving the core, recognizable elements of AOL, which conveyed warmth and optimism.

The original logo triangle contained two swirl shapes moving in a closed circle. Desgrippes Gobé converted the circle into a globe, making it an intuitive symbol of the Internet's multiple benefits—as a roundtable where people come together, as an endless source of power and energy, and as a universe of new experiences and discoveries.

They also gave the logo a three-dimensional quality, with rounded corners and corresponding highlights, to lift it off the background. As Gobé explains, "This was appropriate because we live in a wireless society. We float in space and have the freedom to reach new dimensions. This logo also exists in space. It signals that the brand is moving in new directions. It invites you in and takes you to a different place."

The typography was updated with very simple, light letterforms that convey warmth, optimism, and modernity. The signature is clean, well defined, and it stands out among other competitive logos in cyberspace and in the media. The three-dimensionality of the logo and its inviting but progressive letterforms were critical to aligning the logo with the new positioning. These attributes send out the message: It's not about AOL; it's about the consumer.

From Retail Expression to Packaging Design—and Beyond

Desgrippes Gobé supported the logo's message with an entire visual system that signaled change and resonated with both AOL management and consumers. One of the most innovative elements of the program was the parallel creation of a retail expression for the brand that would bring a heightened level of sensory experiences to the AOL-consumer relationship. Desgrippes Gobé designed an AOL experiential store in New York City that contains a "sound studio" where people can listen to music and an "electronic bar" with computers for sending email or photos—taken in the store—to friends and family. Some of the photos were used to build a mosaic of faces that is mounted on a wall in the store and is also reiterated in the new visual system. On a company brochure, for example, you see a checkerboard of photographs of people from all walks of life, children, pets, and travel destinations.

This gives the brand the sense that it is tapped into a network of people around the world. "By sharing your face in the store, you are showing you're a part of a much larger community," says Gobé. "A huge part of the Internet is a sense of community."

When asked how consumers responded to AOL's new brand identity, Gobé remarked, "People's responses were truly positive. They acknowledged the changes but also expressed that they looked forward to participating in new experiences with the brand. AOL is above all a harmony brand, and the brand strategy as expressed in its 'Ten Commitments'—part of AOL's promise of service to members—clearly emphasizes how it is a brand of the community first. In fact, commitment number one is 'AOL will always help our members feel safe and secure.' Security on the Internet is a main concern of users today, and the brand's new positioning speaks to this and makes customer safety and support a priority. For this and many other reasons, people are happy to have an advocate in AOL again."

The ultimate positioning and visual identity were developed and approved, and the new identity was launched in advertising in 2004. But brand development does not stop there. As part of its ongoing relationship with AOL, Desgrippes Gobé not only implemented the company's revitalized brand positioning, brand architecture, and visual identity but also provided company-wide training to align employee behavior with the new brand strategy. Employees, then, act as an extension of the brand's new friendlier attitude.

People photographs collaged onto a wall mural in the AOL headquarters in Dulles, Virginia, highlight the company's new connection with customers and communicates that the brand is tapped into a network of people around the world.

Desgrippes Gobé designed an AOL experiential store in New York City that contains a "sound studio" (bottom right) where people can listen to music and an "electronic bar" (top and bottom left) with computers for sending email or photos—taken in the store—to friends and family.

AOL RED

The reimagining of the AOL RED visual identity began in Summer 2005 with a fairly straightforward request: to replace the "old triangle" in the RED logo with the new graphic from the recently redesigned AOL logo. As a service of AOL targeted solely at teens, RED needed an updated look to stay visually connected to its parent brand.

However, as the AOL business strategy evolved toward a focus on advertising, RED followed suit. Plans were quickly underway to expand RED to the Web and open its doors to a much wider audience, with a focus on delivering a broad range of original, cutting-edge content and services.

The Challenge

Desgrippes Gobé took the opportunity to totally redesign the RED logo and its visual identity to more accurately represent the service over the next phase of its growth as well as generate some real noise and excitement in the marketplace.

The key objective was to communicate that while RED is part of the AOL branded network, it is also a distinct, highly customized service. In other words, it's "not your parents' AOL." The challenge, therefore, was to create a logo and an evolved identity that would be meaningful and relevant to a sharp and oftentimes fickle online teen audience. The RED visual identity needed to be current, fresh, inspired, and witty—all while maintaining a clear emotional and visual connection to the AOL brand and its core attributes.

The RED Logo

After a great deal of experimentation and exploration, Desgrippes Gobé created a unique, quirky logo consisting of the main graphic expression (affectionately called "the Rabbit") and the RED wordmark. A series of twelve alternate graphics make up a family of expressions that reflect the ever-changing moods and energy of the teen audience while still communicating RED's core positioning and values. The logo and visual identity as a whole have been designed as a flexible system that can be extended and adapted across a variety of applications and touch points.

When tested with the target, the Rabbit logo was the clear choice. Teens noted as "attention-grabbing," "unique," "fun," and "cool," and immediately recognized within it a platform for their own self-expression and individualism.

The main RED logo is made up of the primary expression and the RED wordmark. The primary expression was designed to have a good-natured but neutral feel as it most often represents the personality of the RED brand.

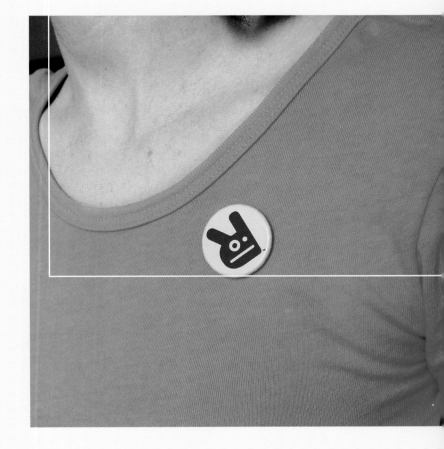

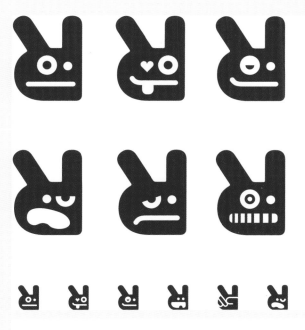

A family of secondary expressions was created to complement the primary expression and provide RED users with opportunities for engagement and customization.

This T-shirt, button, and "website" were created as mock illustrations to demonstrate the RED identity system in context and inspire the development and design of the RED Web site and ancillary promotional activities.

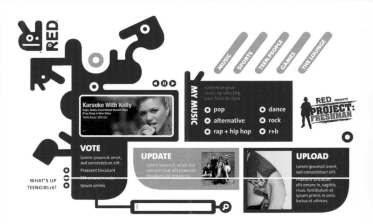

AQUA SAMOA

Aqua Samoa is a deep-sea diving school on the island of Samoa, a country well known for its pristine underwater sites and contained tourist infrastructure, which makes it a favorite destination of sports enthusiasts and nature lovers. One of the first deep-sea diving schools on the island, Aqua Samoa needed to brand its services to promote its incomparable location and inspire its team of teachers and professionals around a common identity. Desgrippes Gobé saw in this small assignment an opportunity to design a visual identity that could help the business stand out as an island attraction. With limited funds and big ambitions, the school convinced Desgrippes Gobé to take on the design of its visual identity, feeling that its image was critical to its growth and to people's perceptions of its unique offering.

Because the school had very few funds for advertising, Desgrippes Gobé recommended that the school's clients carry out the communications themselves. All the company needed was a new logo that was highly visible. If the Aqua Samoa logo could be recognized in the millions of photographs visitors to the island took home with them each year and shared with friends over the Internet, then the school did not need to spend money on a full advertising campaign. The strategy was to create a logo that not only identified the company but that also could appear on T-shirts—a promotion that tourists would wear on the island as well as when they returned home—and in tourist's vacation photos.

The logo needed to make people dream of the magical destination of Samoa and inspire them to discover the thrill and natural beauty of deep-sea diving. Desgrippes Gobé presented five designs inspired by the colorful and optimistic energy of the South Pacific. The wave logo—a representation of a wave inside a circle, symbolizing the Earth—was adopted because of its immediate energy, vitality, and visual strength.

Photographs taken underwater are incorporated into the designs to draw the viewer into the world of deep-sea diving, with its exotic landscape, luminous blue water, and, of course, its schools of multicolored fish.

By creating a logo that not only identified the company but also could appear on T-shirts or other take-home items such as wet suits, the mark could serve as a promotional vehicle.

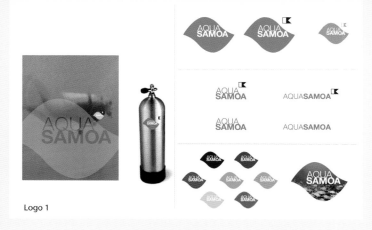

Logo 1

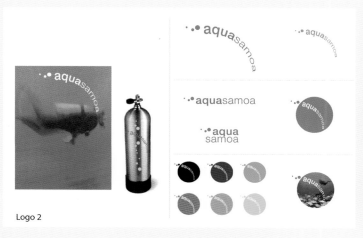

Logo 2

The logo designs Desgrippes Gobé generated for Aqua Samoa play with the look of letterforms contorted under water, floating up like air bubbles to the surface, as well as curved forms evocative of waves, water drops, the Sun, and the Earth.

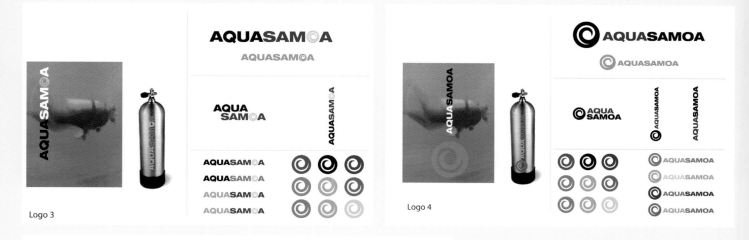

Logo 3

Logo 4

An image of a diver immersed in the beautiful, exotic world of the deep conveys the activity's mysterious and adventuresome spirit and breathtaking scenery.

Logo 5

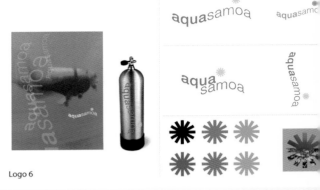

Logo 6

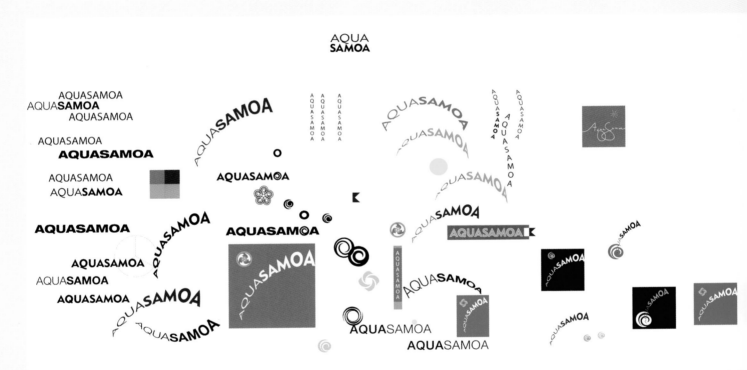

AQUARIUS

Coca-Cola launched its new sports drink, Aquarius, in Belgium in 1993, and since then the category has been growing exponentially. By 2002, Coca-Cola wanted to bring back a sense of stature to Aquarius, whose identity had become out of date, in order to compete with the new additions to the market. Desgrippes Gobé stepped in to refresh the brand through a reinvigorated positioning and visual identity.

The objective was to generate graphic design that was in line with the updated Aquarius positioning and brand vision and that would also be applicable to a diverse set of packagings (from PET bottles to cans), as Coca-Cola intended to extend Aquarius into new product concepts, ranges, and flavors (such as Aquana and Aquarius Perform).

Know Your Customer

The new brand positioning presented Aquarius as a competent sports partner for the recreational athlete who enjoys sports activities as fun, social events. "For the Aquarius customer, playing sports is a chance to use his body and mind, build his capabilities, but also to have fun, feel alive, release tension, and connect with friends," says art director Brigitte Evrard. Desgrippes Gobé capitalized on the brand's equities of being a rapid thirst quencher that replenishes the body, sustaining effort and aiding recovery while also providing a unique, delicious taste. Important to the brand positioning as well was Aquarius's ingredient story, rich in vitamins and mineral salts that help to bring the athlete back into balance.

The design solution is attractive and distinctive compared to other sports drinks, with a high impact on the shelf. The graphics highlight the brand's functional benefits, while the vibrant colors and active, "swoosh" lines speak about hydration, healthiness, and athletic competence.

Playing off the central capital A of the original design, the new graphics bring even more dynamism to this recognizable element by making it part of the design itself. The A divides the label in half to give it graphic duality and balance and to lift the emotional energy upward, balancing the two halves of the design as it balances their corporate versus emotional significations. The left half expresses the "head" aspects of Aquarius, its equities and identity that represent the brand as a whole, while the right half links the product to its different incarnations according to flavor and style.

The original Aquarius bottle (top) featured a large capital A in its design but did not use the entire label to its advantage. Desgrippes Gobé kept the familiar A in its new design (bottom), using it to dynamically divide the composition in half. On the left side the identity of the brand, the Aquarius blue, is consistent on all labels, while the right side of the A provides an opportunity to distinguish the flavor and attributes of the particular drink.

Contemporary bottle designs were created evoking the cutting-edge sports culture the beverage caters to.

The energetic swoosh line catalyzed by the central A is carried through in the secondary packaging.

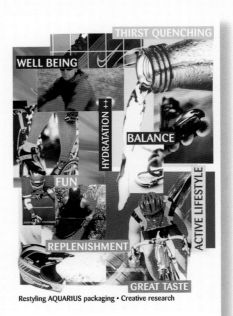

Restyling AQUARIUS packaging • Creative research

An Aquarius storyboard provides inspiration for the brand's new packaging.

AVALON

Most nightclubs come in and out of fashion, but a few stay on as landmarks of a city's nightlife, past, present, and future. The Limelight in Manhattan was the most famous remnant of New York City's Studio 54 days, and so when it came time to conceive of a new club in its place, its owners had the opportunity to play with history. Desgrippes Gobé was hired on to reinvent the Limelight as Avalon, a stylish, multi-room nightspot with all of the cachet of the former establishment but with some extraordinary additions in terms of the interior design and architecture. The main objective was to transform the infamous neo-Gothic church (an 1840 creation by Richard Upjohn, the architect of Trinity Church on Wall Street) into an entirely fresh club experience.

Geology of a Nightclub

Desgrippes Gobé wanted to break away from the heavy history of the Limelight and create a space that conveyed a sense of one generation taking over another, freeing itself from the past. In this way, the new design would retain pieces of the prior club—sections of the original brick wall, its Gothic arches and stained-glass windows—while building into them completely new rooms and structural elements. Experiencing Avalon would be much like experiencing the geological excavation of a nightclub, its layers laid bare, offering a vibe rich in texture that blends the past with the future.

The design concept was to highlight the original architecture of the building and create an exciting juxtaposition between what is "original" and what is new, much like the reinvention of the Musée d'Orsay in Paris, which successfully morphs a nineteenth-century train station into a modern-day art museum. The team created wall decorations that peel away like skin to expose the time-rubbed brick walls of the old church interior. Futuristic forms float in space and protrude from the walls as if to demonstrate that a new type of architecture was rapidly sprouting out of the decay.

The entrance to the club retains the Gothic air of the former church, complete with stained-glass windows and original stone walls, while exuding a glamorous vibe of twenty-first-century club culture.

"The idea of dancing in a church isn't taboo anymore. Madonna's 'Like a Prayer' video broke through all that."

—Sam O'Donahue, Design Director, Desgrippes Gobé New York

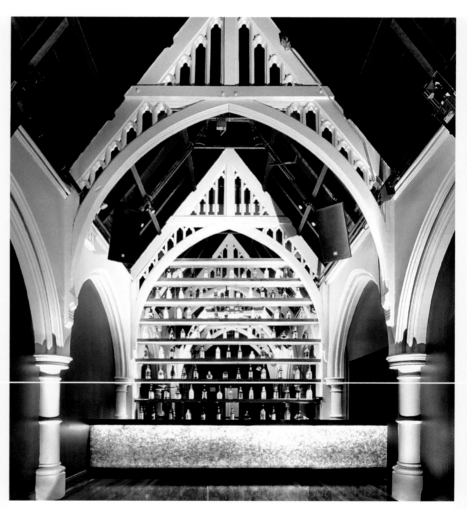

Now that the church has long broken into the nightclub world, lead designer Sam O'Donahue had no problem transforming this once-sacred nave of the church into the main bar, which looks onto the dance floor. He kept the Gothic structures and ornamentation, painting the arches pale blue and placing outdoor accent lights at the base of each column to set the mood.

The Five Elements

Since the building was composed of many rooms, Desgrippes Gobé grouped them under five emotional themes so that no two adjacent rooms would have the same feel. Based on the essential experiences people crave when they go to a club, the themes span from Discovery to Seduction, Fantasy, Energy, and Escape. The designers chose Discovery as the theme for in-between areas, such as corridors or passageways, which all provide vistas onto other spaces and rooms. The Seduction theme was all about voyeurism and was employed in areas off the main dance floor where you could get a drink and look out onto the crowd. Fantasy inspired completely over-the-top spaces, rooms that were always unexpected. Energy infuses the fresh, rhythmic vibe of the music and light on the dance floors. Finally, Escape was about getting away from it all, tucking into quieter corners where you could sit, have a conversation, and do what you like.

Different thematic zones were visually linked by the designers' incorporation of curved details, such as arched ceilings and molded walls, fluidly defying the rigid, cold, and murky interior of the previous club. The rooms pulsed with a new lighting design and vibrant, eye-popping color that emulated the dazzling beauty of illuminated stained glass, giving the club its of-the-moment feel. "The idea of dancing in a church isn't taboo anymore. Madonna's 'Like a Prayer' video broke through all that," says Sam O'Donahue, who led the design concept for the project. It is equally no longer taboo to strip away the old and the heavy to make room for exciting design and an irreplaceable experience.

The infamous neo-Gothic church on the corner of West 20th Street and Sixth Avenue in Manhattan (created by architect Richard Upjohn in 1840) has been home to the world-renowned Limelight of the city's Studio 54 days and housed Club Avalon.

What is unique about the redesign of the club is its ability to incorporate the old into the new. The ticket counter is created out of completely futuristic, curved forms illuminated by space-station-blue lighting, while the original brick walls of the church interior poke through, creating friction between past, present, and future.

Top left: Desgrippes Gobé retained certain interior elements of the church and completely exploded others. One of the club's many passageways provides views onto other levels as well as vantages through walls into rooms beyond.

Center left: One bar area exudes nothing but a modern, chic vibe, countering the curving lines of other spaces as well as the older elements of the original interior with sharp edges and recessed lighting.

Bottom left: Desgrippes Gobé incorporated vastly different materials, from the original brick to stone, drywall, aluminum, and hardwood flooring. The main bar is faced in translucent silver mica and topped with black resin, contrasting daringly with the walnut floors. The ceiling above this end of the bar has been smoothed into a futuristic curve.

Top right: Private rooms with red interiors are housed within electrified walls of white light. Glossy black floors provide contrast as well as a means of reflection.

Bottom right: Carrying on the space-age theme into quieter corners, the designers created a pod-shaped room lined with cushioned brown walls that blend seamlessly into banquette seating. The gateway is illuminated by a polka-dot wall of light evocative of contemporary art.

BANANA REPUBLIC

The apparel retailer Banana Republic saw its personal-care business as an underleveraged opportunity both to grow sales and to deepen its relationship with core customers by adding a dimension of sensuality and crave-worthiness to the brand.

With this opportunity in mind, Banana Republic engaged Desgrippes Gobé as well as Interparfums to develop a comprehensive personal-care line that would simultaneously launch families of fine-fragrance, bath and body, and home products. Desgrippes Gobé was commissioned to develop the positioning strategy, naming, brand architecture, and all primary and secondary packaging.

The Banana Republic Strategy

The brand strategy builds upon the rich heritage of the Banana Republic brand, celebrating the spirit of adventure and discovery that had been so integral when the company originally launched its apparel line more than twenty years ago.

Inspired by diverse and authentic experiences housed under a common roof of uncommonly sensuous beauty, the collection is sophisticated but not complicated or pretentious. Fragrance products such as Jade, Rosewood, and Alabaster, for women, and Black Walnut and Slate, for men, provide customers with a soulful, textured experience that both reflects the store environment and adds to it.

From naming to packaging design, the creative work leverages the concepts of combination and tension. "We drew from the world of luxurious materials, combining rich textures and colors to achieve a collection that is at once carefully considered, varied yet harmonious, and made to inspire the senses," says David Israel, executive creative director.

Adventures in Product Launching

Interparfums incorporated a number of innovations into the technical aspects of the primary and secondary packaging, from the glass weight to the innovative light-diffracting tube in the pump-assembly, making Banana Republic the first company to bring this innovation to the North American market.

"We drew from the world of luxurious materials, combining rich textures and colors to achieve a collection that is at once carefully considered, varied yet harmonious, and made to inspire the senses."

—David Israel, Executive Creative Director, Desgrippes Gobé New York

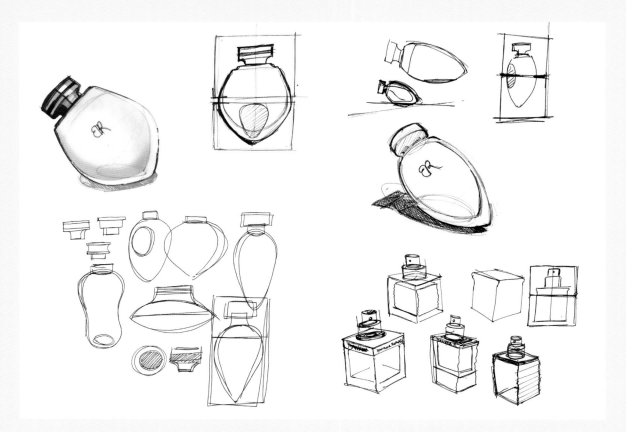

The challenge was to produce the secondary packaging for the 100ml and 50ml fragrances within a short designated time period and the right budget. "We had to find a solution in the secondary packaging that would deliver the concept through the weight and luxury of the look and feel in a cost effective manner," explains 3D creative director Sam O'Donahue.

The product launch was one of the most ambitious personal-care launches in specialty-retail history. In just eleven months, three companies came together to reimagine and reinvent the creative process in order to bring the more than forty new products from concept to shelf. (The industry standard to launch just one new fragrance is twelve to eighteen months.)

The work was a monumental achievement. "It took seven visionary decision makers, seventy-one bicoastal meetings, eleven months of intensive work, and last but not least, an awe-inspiring quantity of stamina, passion, creativity, hard-nosed pragmatism, and fanatical dedication," adds Renée Peet, senior director of brand strategy. No wonder.

BATH & BODY WORKS

When first introduced on the market, Bath & Body Works products were an instant craze among teenage girls, who loved the brand's fruit-scented soaps, lotions, candles, and other bathroom luxuries. Excited to break into a new buying category, these core customers filled their shower baskets with multiple selections from the brand's full range of products, and soon Bath & Body Works became a household name. But everyone grows up, and it became time for the brand to shift its focus to older, more sophisticated shoppers—those women who are no longer girls but who still appreciate fresh scents, homemade quality, and healthy living. Bath & Body Works decided to launch new product lines that would expand the brand beyond the bath and into the home.

One Voice

When Desgrippes Gobé took on the project of reconceptualizing Bath & Body Works' brand presence, retail environments, and product lines, the first step was to clarify the product offering and create store signage that facilitated navigation. An important element in this was the development of a new program that both informed and enhanced customers' shopping experience. The goal was to unify Bath & Body Works' products and retail environment with one coherent voice and feel. Within that "voice" would be variations on the overall theme of Midwestern freshness and creativity in the home, including home products such as the Gingham and Joyful Garden lines.

Through Brand Focus, the team developed a positioning for the brand that evoked the feeling and emotion of the American heartland and its unique celebration of natural colors, flavors, fruits, and flowers. "Kate," an imaginary woman, was created as the store's proprietor—her vision, taste, and lifestyle helped to guide the Brand Focus. As a midwestern woman over thirty, Kate thrived on creativity and bringing an atmosphere of well-being into her home. "We followed this imaginary person to her favorite farm stands, where the freshest produce could be selected and purchased, and created a brand concept based on the strong sense of American nostalgia found there," Gobé explains.

The Scent of Gingham

Desgrippes Gobé positioned the Gingham fragrance line as a continuation of Bath & Body Works' refined theme of wholesome, natural beauty inspired by life in the American heartland. The line would make a strong visual statement that answered the needs of an authentic, natural woman who has a sense of fashion but is not trendy. The team created a full collection of personal-care products using natural ingredients grown in the Midwest. The design strategy was to translate the traditional country pattern of gingham into a fresh, appealing lifestyle statement, using vibrant blues and crisp whites.

Gingham brings the purity and authenticity of the American heartland to cologne, shower gel, lotion, and bath crystals. Its simple blue-and-white checkered pattern reflects the natural appeal of country living. The gingham-patterned box, identified by its hand-scripted label, opens to reveal yellow polka dots and an apricot-colored lining. The packaging for the foaming bath oil crystals was inspired by an old-fashioned milk bottle, and the soap is embossed with a basket-weave pattern. The cologne's glass bottle guarantees purity with gently rounded shoulders and a "foot" to give it a chunky, homespun feel.

"The return to a simpler time and place makes Gingham timeless and familiar," adds Gobé. Gingham was introduced to the press in mid-June 1993 during a picnic lunch in Central Park in New York City, a fitting backdrop for the new products. When it was released in stores two months later, the gingham look also set the tone for the cheery and informal retail concept Desgrippes Gobé developed for Bath & Body Works stores. The classic, familiar qualities of the Gingham line extend into the store displays, which were reconceived as farm-stand shelves offering a bountiful selection of all-natural, "homegrown" products. The team culled images from old country-market signage that it

The Gingham line makes a strong visual statement with its simple blue-and-white checker pattern, bringing the purity and authenticity of the American heartland to products such as cologne, shower gel, body lotion, and bath crystals. Packaging for the bath crystals was inspired by an old-fashioned milk bottle, while the soap is embossed.

"The customer, whom we called 'Kate', is a midwestern woman over thirty who thrives on creativity and bringing an atmosphere of well-being into her home. We followed this imaginary person to her favorite farm stands, where the freshest produce could be selected and purchased, and created a brand concept based on the strong sense of American nostalgia found there."

—Marc Gobé

then incorporated into the retail environments to recreate the experience of stopping by a roadside stand to buy local produce.

Joyful Garden

The aim of Joyful Garden was to invent a Bath & Body Works toiletries line that echoed the brand's existing equities while also appealing to a more sophisticated woman. With Joyful Garden, Bath & Body Works wanted to meet the needs of customer, who seek new and more mature scents for their bath and body-care products. The line also allowed the brand to expand its customer base to include older women.

The positioning strategy for the new line focused on relaxation, soothing moments, and escapes. "Joyful Garden is reminiscent of a tranquil place where today's modern woman can reclaim her balance and reset her priorities by pampering herself," says Gobé. Three soft fragrances were created to echo the positioning: Stolen Moments, Calming Waters, and Flower Walk. The bottle designs for the fragrances have a simple, organic look to them, and were developed with special materials and textures to feel soft and smooth to the touch. Decorated with elegant watercolor illustrations, the bottles also incorporate touches of poetic copy.

Three theme fragrances for the Joyful Garden line—Stolen Moments, Calming Waters, and Flower Walk—echo the brand positioning. The bottle designs are simple and organic, just like the scents themselves.

The iconic Bath & Body Works bottle anchors the packaging narrative for the brand.

The bottle designs for the Stress Relief line cater to a slightly older and more sophisticated customer who wants to bring a natural-based aesthetic into her home.

The Gingham cologne bottle promises country purity with gently rounded shoulders and a flared bottom to give it a chunky, homespun feel. Secondary packaging also mirrors the old-fashioned box designs with classic striped and checkered patterning.

The clean and fresh simplicity of the Face line was a natural complement to the existing products and allowed Bath & Body Works to extend its products into the skin care area.

The Bath & Body Works cosmetics line caters to the contemporary woman who favors simplicity and no-nonsense living.

BONACTIVE

Standing out as a water brand today is no easy task, as countless beverage makers vie for openings within the category. The Coca-Cola Company commissioned Desgrippes Gobé to create a brand identity for Bonactive, an isotonic water drink that is a line extension of Bonaqua, the company's popular mineralized water in Hong Kong and Macau. To differentiate Bonactive from the original brand and compete with other isotonic drinks, Desgrippes Gobé tried to bring a more sportive feel to the Bonactive brand through naming and packaging design.

Water Power

With Bonaqua's high brand recognition already established, Desgrippes Gobé's design strategy for the new water was to build upon the Bonaqua equities while adding a new twist, beginning with the brand name. The team invented Bonactive, connecting the drink to the parent brand while establishing its unique identity—one dynamically linked to fast-paced, youthful, and active lifestyles. By capitalizing on Bonaqua's success in Hong Kong and Macau and at the same time building a strong contrast between the two products, the brand could take the lead in a competitive niche market of sports waters.

For the new package design, Desgrippes Gobé brought over the blue color as well as the snow-capped mountain motif so evocative of purity and freshness from the Bonaqua label. From here, the designs diverge. The team deepened the blue in the Bonactive label to make it more forceful and energetic than the paler, more passive blue of the original. They then added metallic effects to give the design its athletic zeal and to signal that Bonactive provided more than just refreshment but also the electrolyte replenishment so desired after exertion at work or play.

Even more dynamic is the Bonactive logo symbol, which combines an arrow and cursor shape that circles the brand name and ultimately forms the A and the V, directing the eye back into the logo while also communicating the uplifting qualities of the drink and giving the packaging a sense of energy and action. The circular motion also signifies replenishment and revitalization, again setting Bonactive apart from the more natural feel of the original brand.

The Bonactive extension has been a great market success, even exceeding Coca-Cola's expectations for the brand, and has become a leading contender among the most popular and established isotonic drinks. "It's remarkable what design—in the service of adding energy and emotion to a brand—can do," comments Paul Vickers, who led the design project.

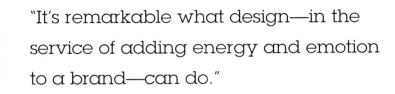

"It's remarkable what design—in the service of adding energy and emotion to a brand—can do."

—Paul Vickers, Regional Creative Director,
Desgrippes Gobé Hong Kong

The final bottle and can designs blend the new Bonactive logo into the surrounding imagery of snow-capped peaks. The whole has a cohesive as well as energetic feel, with dynamic, eye-catching contrast between dark blue and white.

The design team played with different solutions for integrating the Bonactive label into the background imagery and bottle shape.

The Bonactive logo conveys the beverage's sportive, high-energy attributes through the two arrow shapes that grow out of and feed into the wordmark in perpetual motion, giving momentum to the composition. The movement is echoed in the background, where the mountain-peak shapes of the logo image become tiny arrows circling in the same clockwise direction.

The Bonactive bottle structure was designed with an angular body for ease of grip. Desgrippes Gobé conceived background imagery evocative of alpine light and scenery.

BOUCHERON

When one thinks luxury, a flurry of images comes to mind: sumptuous décor, shimmering jewelry, richly adorned furniture. Today, none of these represent luxury in and of itself; luxury is expressed in a more subtle and discreet way. "When I was contacted to create the first perfume for this internationally renowned French jeweler," recalls Joël Desgrippes, "I spent a lot of time with Alain Boucheron to grasp the style of this more than one-hundred-year-old house. It was the beginning of an osmosis between the craft of the jeweler and the craft of the perfumer during ten years of intense collaboration with Claude Le Rouzic, then Boucheron's CEO. It was a very successful alchemy."

Desgrippes Gobé's objective was to develop the reputation of the brand through the creation of unique objects that only Boucheron could create. The firm then created a complete range of perfumes for women and men by tapping the world of fine jewelry.

The Jeweler's Perfume

First, Desgrippes Gobé designed the brand symbol around the icon of the Vendôme column in the Place Vendôme in Paris. Not only is the column a symbol of France's stormy nineteenth-century history (erected by Napoleon in 1810, it was torn down by Communards, led by painter Gustave Courbet, in 1871, and restored a few years later), but the Place Vendôme is also where the most famous jewelry and luxury brands in the world first set up shop. The Vendôme column, posed as a backdrop in advertisements for the new Boucheron perfume, evokes the brand's strong French heritage and prestige as the first jeweler to establish itself on the square.

"By using the sensorial universe of precious stones like sapphires, diamonds, or pearls, we have been able to create a unique style for the perfume that is recognized everywhere in the world," Joël explains.

The first Boucheron perfume drew its inspiration from the shape of a ring bejeweled with a "precious stone" cap. This initial creation has been the symbol of the brand and its

The final design for the original Boucheron fragrance blends the shape of a ring with its precious-stone setting into the shape of a high-end perfume bottle. The lines are simple and clean, conveying the upscale, haute-couture world of its maker.

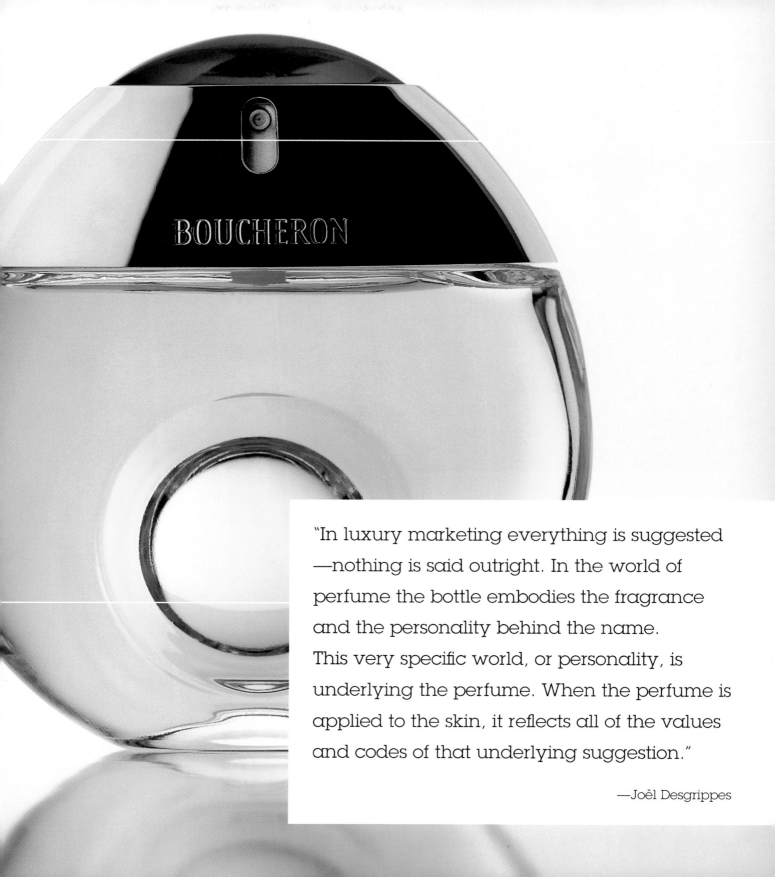

BOUCHERON

"In luxury marketing everything is suggested
—nothing is said outright. In the world of
perfume the bottle embodies the fragrance
and the personality behind the name.
This very specific world, or personality, is
underlying the perfume. When the perfume is
applied to the skin, it reflects all of the values
and codes of that underlying suggestion."

—Joël Desgrippes

For the Jaipur scent, the bottle design takes its inspiration from classic Indian jewelry, here a cut-crystal bracelet. Gold and sapphire elements tie the bottle into the original ring concept.

industry ever since. The line was expanded to include other symbolic objects such as the bracelet and the pendant. But with the introduction of the Jaipur scent, the brand really took off: the bottle design was inspired by a chiseled-crystal bracelet adorned with a sapphire-blue precious stone. Meanwhile, Boucheron's specialty watches directly inspired designs for the men's fragrances. In this way, a whole new line of objects based on classic jewelry designs was created in the ten years Desgrippes Gobé worked with the brand.

From Concept to Universe

These designs extended to each new fragrance addition. The link to the feminine is integral to the perfume's story, as it magically connects the purity and the voluptuousness of a jewel to the woman who wears it. All of the Boucheron fragrances, themselves precious, are captured inside a jewel; the fragrance becomes the treasure at the heart of the gem, while the gem surrounds the fragrance, refracting light, inviting you in. Each gesture means an experience leading to the discovery of the fragrance.

Just as Boucheron represents some of the highest-quality jewelry in the world, now through its fragrance line it also represents the highest-quality perfumes, each with its own identity and legend.

The Jaipur men's fragrance distinguishes itself
from the feminine curves of the women's perfume bottle with square shoulders and strong
brushed-silver elements.

For the men's line, the bottle shape echoes the ring design of the women's fragrance,
while giving it a more structured, masculine presence.

BROOKS BROTHERS

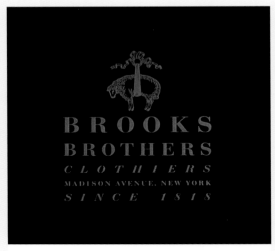

The shopping bag is authoritative and impactful, with turquoise diagonal stripes on the side panels to reinforce the connection to the brand's classic rep tie.

Branding at first might not seem to apply to a time-tested name such as Brooks Brothers, the classic men's clothing brand that originated on New York City's Upper East Side. The clothier has such a distinctive style and clientele that there would seem little point in rebranding it: everyone knows who and what Brooks Brothers is. But in fact, as times change, so must brands. The key for a brand such as Brooks Brothers was to catch up with current trends and attract a new generation of younger customers without alienating its existing clients, who in most cases have grown up with the brand and therefore respect it.

"Therein lie endless opportunities and challenges," points out Marc Gobé. "Even a company such as Brooks Brothers, which serves a predominantly conservative clientele of a certain age, can think about how some younger segment of the population gets inspired and transforms that meaning into a different brand message." Desgrippes Gobé was brought in to revitalize the Brooks Brothers brand and give it a more contemporary image. The task was to create a new identity and packaging system, representing the first wave of the brand's repositioning.

The Coolness of the Golden Fleece

For the new logo, the design team chose to feature bright-blue lettering on Brooks Brothers' classic dark-navy-blue background. The mixture of type sizes and letter spacing was meant to look like an updated version of a classic bookplate that would appear in the front of a hand-bound book. The logo retains the long-used Golden Fleece icon, the profile of a sheep being lifted up in a luxurious ribbon, but in a lively rendition that looks more energetic. The brand name is also executed in bolder capital letters, replacing the old fussy script, while the word "Clothiers" echoes the heritage of the brand. Desgrippes Gobé created starker, more impactful shopping bags featuring jazzy turquoise diagonal stripes on the side panels that reinforce the brand's trademark rep tie.

The resulting design takes an old and somewhat stuffy identity and evolves it to communicate both a modern and sophisticated image appropriate to the way men and women, both young and old, live today.

"If a brand does not deliver on an emotional aspiration, customers will adapt or appropriate brands for their own purposes," explains Gobé. "We think of our products in narrow-minded ways, but brand meanings can evolve; they can be adapted and reinterpreted to meet individual styles. Brooks Brothers cool? Absolutely."

The secondary packaging retains the simple, classic air of the Brooks Brothers' style while incorporating slightly jazzier elements of bright blue and diagonal rep-tie stripes.

BROOKS BROTHERS
CLOTHIERS
MADISON AVENUE, NEW YORK
SINCE 1818

The new logo features bright blue lettering on Brooks Brothers' classic dark-navy background. Keeping the long-used Golden Fleece icon, the design team created a more lively and energetic rendition.

"We think of our products in emotional ways, but brand meanings can evolve; they can be adapted and reinterpreted to meet individual styles."

—Marc Gobé

CJ

Since 1953, the Cheil Jedang company ("Cheil" meaning the "best" and the "first"; "Jedang" meaning "sugar refining") has firmly established itself as a reliable provider of high-quality food products both in Korea and abroad. Following its separation from Samsung in 1993, it began to expand its scope of operations into new high-growth businesses such as media, entertainment, and home-shopping cable channels. Because of this, the company needed to adopt a new corporate identity, one that expressed its widening horizons. Desgrippes Gobé was hired to create a logical and flexible corporate identity for the Cheil Jedang group that was both powerful and representative of the company's unique culture and long-lived commitment to providing quality products and services.

A Company Reborn

The first major step the design team took was to recommend a corporate name change: from Cheil Jedang to CJ. This way, the company would no longer be immediately associated with food products, but own a unique, more friendly set of initials that signified its enterprise as a whole. Next came the definition of the group's brand architecture—the system of brand elements that would communicate the breadth and character of CJ's subsidiary brands. Finally, the team fashioned a new corporate logo for the company.

"We call the new CJ logo 'nature in motion,'" says Elie Hasbani, lead designer on the project. "We created a natural and organic shape that draws upon the imagery of leaves and flower petals to represent the fact that CJ is blossoming, opening up to the outside world." Set against a crisp white background and juxtaposed with the clear, black letterforms of the company's new corporate name, the logo speaks to the group's new start as a global business in a world of yet-to-be-discovered consumers, both inside and outside of Korea.

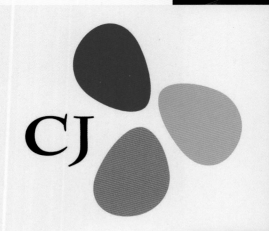

The primary colors of the new logo represent a fresh start for CJ. The circular motion of the shapes and their proximity yet distinction from one another represent the company's business model of different components working together yet also branching out into a range of market segments. The white background and stark black lettering serve to highlight the colorful palette.

The logo comes alive to identify a CJ truck.

"We call the new CJ logo 'nature in motion.'
We created a natural and organic shape
that draws upon the imagery of leaves and
flower petals to represent the fact that CJ is
blossoming, opening up to the outside world."

—Elie Hasbani, Lead Designer, Desgrippes Gobé Paris

Natural Motion

The primary color palette—red, yellow, and blue—represents the core of life, a new beginning. The petal shapes also invoke a child's first finger paints, with which all other colors can be made mixing any two together. At the same time, red and blue connect the design back to CJ's heritage, and a rich yellow is added to enhance the natural feeling. "Here yellow means life, something more human and close to people," explains Hasbani. "It means proximity, as CJ has a wide range of business activities that touch the consumer in his or her everyday life."

The three shapes represent CJ's corporate universe, which is made up of CJ as a company, its customers, and its staff. The circular motion of the shapes and their proximity yet distinction from one another represent the natural evolution of and constant interaction between CJ's different business segments. The ultimate effect of the new identity is one of radiance, balance, openness, friendliness, and the sense that this is a very human company that also strives for perfection.

With its petal shapes of blue, red, and yellow, the logo invokes children's first finger paints, which can be mixed . together to create virtually any other color. A CJ advertisement plays with this idea, conveying the company's new beginnings and friendly, more human nature.

The simple yet vibrant logo stands out against the company's modern office building and creates a striking billboard.

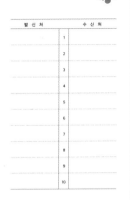

CJ주식회사
서울시 중구 중림동 441
한국경제신문사빌딩 (우)100-791
Tel: 02 6740-1114

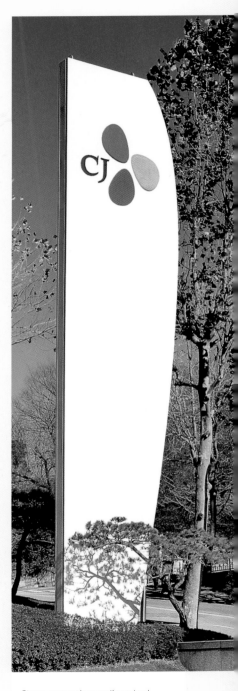

장 은 영
수석 디자이너
디자인센터

CJ주식회사
서울특별시 중구 중림동 441번지
한국경제신문빌딩 7층 (우)100-791
Tel: 02 6740-0558 Fax: 02 6740-1041~42
Mobile: 019-213-8698
eMail: cey0126@cj.net

Eun-Yong Chang
Art Director
DESIGN CENTER

CJ Corp.
7F, Hankyung Bldg. 441, Chunglim-dong,
Chung-ku, Seoul, 100-791, Korea
Tel: 82 2 6740-0558 Fax: 82 2 6740-1041~42
Mobile: 82 19-213-8698
eMail: cey0126@cj.net

Stationery designs take advantage of the clean white
page, against which the colorful logo pops out.

Signage expands upon the natural
curves within the logo to give the overall
brand presence its more humanistic and
less corporate feel.

CLEAR

"In the post 9/11 era, we had to take new measures to protect ourselves yet not destroy our way of life by strangling the free flow of people and commerce. Somehow, we had to find common sense solutions to security bottlenecks that make everyone a suspect. . . . We needed a fair, sensible way not to treat everyone the same when it comes to terrorism protection."—from Verified Identity Pass, Inc., website

The meaning of security in public spaces and how it is implemented has changed drastically since 9/11. Airport security especially is now more diligent but much less efficient. Every traveler has experienced the enormous security lines, the tedious, invasive checks, the close calls of missing flights, as well as the misses. At the same time, every traveler wants to be safe and wants others to be safe, and he or she is willing to give security a greater presence in their lives. This is why Verified Identity Pass, Inc., an identity credentialing company, has created Clear™, the first national, privately run, pre-screening security program.

"Clear is the smarter way forward for airport security, shifting limited security resources away from lower-risk candidates," says the company's website. "It's basic risk management: someone who is pre-screened is less likely to be a threat than someone who isn't." Members go through an initial application and screening process, then are given a Clear ID card that they can use at Clear security stations at the airport, whisking them into the gate area without any hassle or long waits. Desgrippes Gobé took on the development of Clear's positioning, naming, logo, visual language, and retail identity.

In the Clear

The team brainstormed names for the new program and selected Clear because of what it stands for: the idea that, in risk situations such as travel, people's identities should be clear and easy to read. "More than a name," says Lisa Koenigsberg, Desgrippes Gobé's director of business development, "Clear captures Verified ID's point of view. The name speaks to the company's mission, its product benefits

"Progressive technology and practice is generally met with healthy skepticism. Our challenge with Clear was to communicate 'new' and 'progressive' while reassuring travelers that they could literally trust them with their lives."

–Judd Harner, President, Desgrippes Gobé, New York

of clarity, trust, and ease. Desgrippes Gobé's objective was to convey these benefits visually through every consumer touch point."

Once the team had solved the positioning and naming for the brand, it created a logo and supporting visual language that was then translated into the design of the ID card—the Clear Pass—advertising, company brochures, the business system, and ultimately extended to the design of the first airport location in the Orlando International Airport.

Such a revolutionary concept required an equally groundbreaking, up-to-the-minute design for its products and station environments. Like the Clear Pass itself, the ID stations would communicate the forward thinking behind the concept and its foundation in cutting-edge research and the latest security techniques. The team designed a transparent plastic card with only a pale-blue logo element, the person's name in clean, pale-blue type, and the identity chip showing. The positioning is also brought to life in the design for the check-in stations, incorporating blue-tinted, transparent walls, thin metallic structural elements, and the most advanced computer technology.

Verified Identity is a growing business as well as a developing branding and experience design project. The Clear concept provides a model for future projects in the field that combine graphics with architectural design to create a total brand presence.

The Clear identity card is itself "clear" and simply designed, mirroring the simplified process of identity checking that the program has introduced.

The Clear station is designed to be unobtrusive and easy for passengers to navigate quickly.

ORLANDO IS CLEAR

THE SMARTER WAY FORWARD FOR AIRPORT SECURITY.

To learn how you can travel smarter, visit www.flyclear.com.

CLEAR ORLANDO INTERNATIONAL AIRPORT'S
VERIFIED IDENTITY PASS

CLEAR™

REGISTERED TRAVELER

JAMES S. DOE
075125 54278

Advertising emphasizes the feeling of ease the new identity-check-ing system provides. The distinctive shape of the Clear identity card is echoed in the slogan.

CLUB MED

Since its creation more than fifty years ago, Club Med has been synonymous with dream vacations and travel experiences for singles, couples, and families worldwide. However, the brand imagery grew to be viewed as cliché in recent years, confining the brand to a vacation sector that was no longer unique or desirable. In today's competitive market of luxury hotels, holiday clubs, resorts, and tailored tour packages, Club Med wanted to reposition itself as a valid luxury option, one that provided the exclusive, friendly, and multicultural experiences its customers demanded. With the help of Desgrippes Gobé, Club Med revolutionized its brand territory and visual system to express its new vision of and place in the realm of world tourism.

What Are Your Core Values?

Desgrippes Gobé based its strategy on five fundamental corporate values that are the essence of the brand and the company behind it: multiculturalism, freedom, kindness, responsibility, and a pioneering nature. The designers developed a graphic vocabulary based on these values and their definitions. Multiculturalism means a wealth of influences and an open mind; freedom means energy, pleasure, and enthusiasm; kindness evokes a public-minded spirit, generosity, and a joie de vivre; responsibility suggests professionalism, quality, and service; pioneering nature implies creativity, sophistication, and cutting-edge design.

Just like a person, Club Med has a personality all its own, and it was this personality that had to show itself in every type of communication. To pinpoint the Club Med experience, which is different from that of the traditional travel provider or hotelier, Desgrippes Gobé asked the brand: If you were a person, who would you be? The brand replied with a comprehensive list of personal attributes.

Club Med is an elegant and sophisticated person, never flashy but possessing an individual elegance interested in harmony and enjoying life. She is a creative person who revels in diverse experiences, surprising locations, and seeks out unusual solutions. She is a surprising person, never running out of new ideas, cherishing originality and a zany approach to life. She

is a generous person who is interested in others, a good friend always looking for ways to please those she likes. She is a happy person, optimistic and energetic. And she is a person open to the world, curious about other people and places, who sees the world as an infinite source of discovery and shared moments.

These attributes fed into all graphic communications Desgrippes Gobé created, expressing not only the unique personality of the brand itself but also the personalized interests of Club Med customers.

Friendly Luxury

Desgrippes Gobé's initial design concept revolved around the notion of "friendly luxury"—luxury that is high-class but also gracious, fun, and humanistic, that invents new ways of thinking about vacationing. The Desgrippes Gobé team created an entire new brand universe, complete with refreshed corporate identity, packaging and retail design systems, online presence, environment design and signage, and an integrated global branding program.

"Friendly, upmarket, and multicultural, the Club Med brand is changing, and its visual expression, its graphic universe, is changing with it," says creative director Elie Hasbani. "Club Med has invented a new chemistry: luxury with a human touch, warm and generous, a luxury that is meant to be shared."

The new positioning was consistent with the exceptional locations in which Club Med villages are located. As the villages themselves are Club Med's main message, Desgrippes

Advertising posters play with the traditional horizon line by juxtaposing a clear blue sky with the underwater world of tropical snorkeling.

Collaged graphics for Club Med advertisements combine exterior and interior imagery to create an inside-outside feel, incorporating artistically rendered flower silhouettes to introduce the imaginary element.

Club Med Ψ
IL RESTE TANT DE MONDE À DÉCOUVRIR

Desgrippes Gobé retained the Mediterranean-blue color and trident symbol of the original Club Med logo. The simultaneously relaxed and contemporary typeface conveys a friendly as well as sophisticated attitude.

"For Club Med, we invented the casual luxury resort, what we call 'friendly luxury.'"

—François Caratgé, General Manager, Desgrippes Gobé Paris

Gobé's design allowed the brand to communicate effectively through them. Previously in Club Med communications, the eye was oriented toward the horizon, into the distance, to enhance the beauty of the places where you could go when you chose Club Med. But this was no longer sufficient to define the new positioning, so the team created imaginary horizons—ones that orient viewers inward toward their fantasies as well as open them up to an exterior world without limit.

From the Inside Out

Rich in imagery and gestural details, the graphics range from colorful photographs to hand-drawn renderings. "The whole looks much like a friendly yet stylish invitation to do something, even if it is simply chatting with friends and telling stories," points out Hasbani. "Everything is based on a horizontal plane, from which stories of special moments, exclusive to each person, expand out in all directions. Like visual collages of experiences, the new Club Med communications invite people to create their own dreams."

Frontiers between exterior and interior no longer exist. Juxtaposing glimpses of indoor spaces with outdoor environments, people's faces with natural landscapes, collaged images provide surprising visual interplays. In some pictures, elements cross the horizon line and penetrate other visuals, creating a playful harmony and double take. Both the advertising campaign and the graphic style play on this duality between the exterior world waiting to be explored and the interior world of the imagination, ultimately symbolizing an eagerness to set out and discover not only exceptional sites but also oneself and others.

Colors have been widely diversified to evoke new visual pleasures and flavors and to nourish the imagination, ranging from soft sage green to bright tangerine, meadow yellow, lilac, and crimson. Desgrippes Gobé designated a unique pictogram and color palette for each Club Med village, which in turn ties back into the overall visual system and extends to all signage as well as internal and external communications.

Advertising posters pairing luxurious interior details such as a rich red pillow and antique vase with natural and playful imagery are a fundamental part of the new identity system, juxtaposing interior with exterior, high style with freedom. Tiny silhouettes of people out enjoying life help enliven the composition and create a visual double take.

Each Club Med village has its own visual motif and color palette evocative of its personality. The graphic elements all carry the same sinuous and playful style, while surprising, and hip, color combinations attract the eye and tie back into the overall visual system.

The distinct essences of each Club Med experience are communicated by integrating both outdoor landscapes and interior stylings into the poster's picture plane. The horizon line is played with to create a synergy between extroverted and introverted moments.

Eye-catching vantages in advertisements capture the startling natural beauty waiting to be discovered on a Club Med vacation as well as the quality of its accommodations.

Variations in color palette show the different appearances the logos can make, for Columbus Isle, Otranto, and Peisey-Vallandry.

COCA-COLA

The day Desgrippes Gobé was to meet with top executives at Coca-Cola to pitch for the project of developing the brand's new visual identity system and packaging graphics, the New York office was abuzz with excitement, and nerves. The team had been preparing day and night for this crucial presentation. Representatives from Desgrippes Gobé's offices in Europe and Asia came to lend support and to demonstrate the firm's broad-based commitment to the project. The team suggested that Coca-Cola was an international brand in need of an international design force, and Desgrippes Gobé was just that.

From Corporate to Emotional Identity

Coca-Cola was ideally suited for the emotional brand experience that only Desgrippes Gobé could offer. In the previous two decades, Coca-Cola had successfully implemented a consistent visual identity system across the globe, and its packaging graphic—the contour bottle—was the dominant visual image defining the brand identity in the marketplace. While this monolithic visual identity system did one thing well—it built a uniform consumer impression—it wasn't flexible enough to encompass the full spectrum of consumer needs, emotional states, or communications environments that Coca-Cola reached. Research showed that the brand was lacking personal relevance to consumers, an audience that ranged all the way from the suburban mom to a family at a baseball game to teens at a nightclub. What was more, the brand was losing ground in the crucial youth market, and its imagery was increasingly being viewed as "wallpaper," which, needless to say, did little to stimulate consumption behavior.

"The Coca-Cola project gave us the opportunity to put our emotional branding process into action with a brand that has unrivaled scope for facilitating and benefiting from our methods," says Marc Gobé. "Too often designers and clients mistake branding for a process of ubiquitous communication: in fact, branding always entails a thoughtful, developed deployment that unfolds over time as it expands existing relationships (with consumer and company alike) and builds new ones."

Desgrippes Gobé partnered with Coca-Cola's Global Branding Team to develop a new visual identity system and packaging graphic. Breaking away from the traditional program, Desgrippes Gobé advised that the brand team leverage the packaging graphic and Coke's iconic visual identity as the central theme for all of its presences. The idea was to design a comprehensive emotional identity program that would present the brand to the world in a fresh, dynamic way. The shift from a static corporate identity to a new and exciting emotional identity was the key to the brand's transformation beyond just the color red and typographic script.

"The important step in this project, from an emotional perspective, was to 'observe' the audience we needed to communicate with," explains Gobé. "We had to determine what deep subconscious values young people were looking for. Furthermore, we had to identify which of those the Coke iconography was best positioned to respond to. Understanding how young people live, the music they listen to, the sports they like, and the moments they treasure was crucial. With these answers we began answering the key emotional branding questions: Who are we? Are we loved?

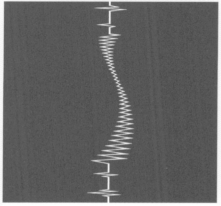

"Gut" graphics feature the dynamic ribbon in innovative contexts evocative of high technology, one using computer-generated pixellation and the other playing with the zig-zags of a frequency line.

"Too often designers and clients mistake branding for a process of ubiquitous communication: in fact, branding always entails a thoughtful, developed deployment that unfolds over time as it expands existing relationships (with consumer and company alike) and builds new ones. Deploying the usual vocabulary of a brand to bring out emotional promises in people is often underplayed in a brand manifestation. Coca-Cola's rich, iconic heritage was brought to life to stimulate new engagement between people and the Coke brand."

—Marc Gobé

The evolution of the Coca-Cola can

What's our passion? Who do we want to share our passion with? Are we believable? From these questions, it is possible to establish an emotional personality that lays the groundwork for an inspired design language."

The next step was to clarify Coca-Cola's brand platform to identify the differentiating elements of the brand and those most linked to driving volume. The Desgrippes Gobé team defined the brand's specific communications objectives in humanizing the brand through their emotional lens while looking at the brand expression through the head (logic), heart (role of the brand in society), and gut (the visual appeal a brand needs to convey) framework. Based on this emotional context, they established visual expressions that would help consumers interact with the brand. Head communications included those places where corporate identification was of the highest priority; heart communications were those that fostered a dialogue with consumers in harmonizing or bonding moments; and gut communications were designed to engage teens and young adults through bold statements and daring, spontaneous energy. Each communications vehicle Coca-Cola used—from corporate signage to fountain cups to kiosks to youth-venue vending machines—was reexamined and reclassified to optimize the brand's ability to create stronger, more relevant connections with consumers.

Crafting the "Feel" of Coca-Cola

The bold task of shaping a new visual, emotive narrative for Coca-Cola excited the Desgrippes Gobé team. The brand already resonated with people in an emotional way, and yet it could do so much more. Desgrippes Gobé wanted to help audiences recognize Coca-Cola as a beacon of optimism and diversity, and such elusive, ethereal sentiments are best conveyed with thoughtful design as the basis for communication. The team's mission was to craft the sensory "feel" of Coca-Cola.

"The evolution of the graphics of a brand is not an unusual thing," states Gobé. "Brand iconographies are updated every so many years. Look and usage varies. Our team knew that our design exploration would have to look beyond the famous contour bottle symbol without losing the importance of such an icon. But such endeavors are a sensitive, intuitive affair: though good research is essential, the right design must come from the heart, the brand community, the best of the

corporate culture. Furthermore, one must keep in mind that the final decision will reshape and redefine each of these sites, becoming a permanent part of the brand legacy."

The new emotional model necessitated a design that responded uniquely to consumers' different life moments. The visual identity would have to be at once unified and adaptable to different communications sites: vending machines, billboards near ski slopes, delivery trucks, sporting events, beaches, nightclubs. Each one of these sites elicits unique expectations and engagements, keeping in mind the limitations of Coca-Cola's Spencerian script font, which loses its identity when translated into such languages as Korean, Chinese, or Arabic. Through meeting these site-specific needs, Desgrippes Gobé could shift the brand's iconography from sameness and ubiquity to dynamic, evolutionary involvement.

Coca-Cola's Graphics Rejuvenated

Bringing meaning to the Coke iconography from an emotional perspective, the Desgrippes Gobé team conducted wide-ranging research into the Coca-Cola brand's rich heritage. Buried deep in the layers of Coke's packaging history were three singular elements that emerged to optimize the physical refreshing nature of the product and its mental "coolness": the "dynamic ribbon," "refreshing bubbles," and the color yellow. The team unanimously felt that the vibrant, energetic "swoosh" of white, inherent to Coke's legacy (having first been introduced in 1969), would be integral to the brand's new visual identity particularly when associated with spirited carbonated bubbles. Incorporating the timeless script logo

The classic contour bottle shape and can with updated labeling featuring both the dynamic ribbon and "Coke yellow" stripe.

A "heart" graphic for the brand evokes the recognizable contour bottle icon in a simple, gestural style.

A "gut" graphic renders the contour bottle out of refreshing water shapes.

"Head" graphics readily identify the brand on the side of a delivery truck and on the side of a building.

"Head" graphics extend to innovative designs for a café table, with a tabletop shaped like a Coca-Cola bottle cap.

A contour bottle created out of bubbles makes an effective "heart" graphic.

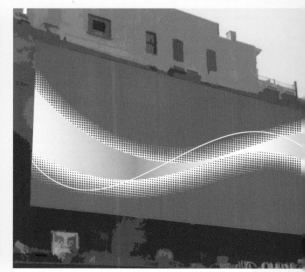

A billboard advertising the brand needs nothing more than a dynamic ribbon to get its message across.

A billboard "gut" graphic signifies the radiant identity of the signature contour bottle with cartoonlike white lines.

with a contemporary and dynamic ribbon design brought the packaging to life, opened up new visual and emotional possibilities for the brand, and demonstrated the brand's willingness to progress with the times.

"Coke yellow" was included in a modest way at first. It was an intuitive idea used to highlight the brand's packaging, making it more energetic, but also reframing and foregrounding Coke's dominant red, which yellow helped to differentiate and make more inspiring. Moreover, the touch of yellow brought a surprising energy and optimism that could enhance the imagery and packaging. Though difficult to measure or demonstrate objectively, the team felt its power. Incidentally, the same can ended up on the cover of Australian *Vogue*, held by a top model/actress. It also graced the runway as a hair ornament in John Galliano's fall 2004 runway show. Coca-Cola had come of age—it had become youthful and "cool"—finally psychologically refreshing.

The little bit of yellow complemented Desgrippes Gobé's biggest idea for the new graphics: the return of the dynamic ribbon. This powerful, abstract visual symbol was

an influential but abandoned icon that the team thought emotionally trumped all others; it suggested the action painting of a Jackson Pollock in its sprawling, dynamic flight, and was a predecessor to the Nike logo. In bringing back the icon, the team felt it would connect sensually and emotionally with today's markets and design languages.

They recommended replacing the contour bottle displayed on the current Coca-Cola can with the dynamic ribbon. When it was launched in the seventies, the ribbon was understood as part of Coca-Cola's growing global brand, since non-Western characters were being introduced onto the can in growing foreign markets and there was a concern that its visual iconography and identity would be diminished. The dynamic ribbon became part of an international graphic language that would be recognized around the globe. In the end, instead of replacing the contour bottle, an updated ribbon was incorporated into the can design, along with the timeless Coca-Cola script logo. The familiar yet newly depicted contour bottle appears on the side panel of the package.

A New Visual System from the Inside Out, and Around the World

The new visual system demonstrated Coca-Cola's newfound flexibility and willingness to adapt effectively to new audiences and environments. In this vein, Desgrippes Gobé created the Coca-Cola Club Can, which extended the brand into the youth scene, where kids out at nightclubs would gravitate toward the new design's cool, cartoony graphics.

With this new flexibility came a critical need for tools that would enable Coca-Cola marketers across the globe to take the communications environment and the customer's emotional states and motivations into account when designing communications materials. Local marketing organizations would need to understand the brand and how to use design and iconography to deepen its relationship with people, while at the same time practicing the highest levels of brand stewardship. Desgrippes Gobé developed a toolkit and Emotional Identity Guidelines to support the worldwide marketing and communications team in rolling out the program. The guidelines prompt the teams to determine their communications goals and objectives, select the appropriate emotional connection level, and choose from a library of graphics offered under each level. This new system ensures that marketers around the world choose the most effective graphics every time.

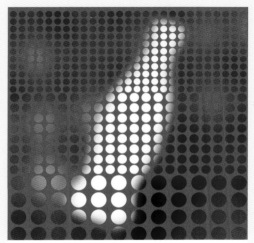

A "gut" graphic featuring the contour bottle.

The immediately recognizable Coca-Cola script cleverly forms the contour bottle icon in this "heart" graphic.

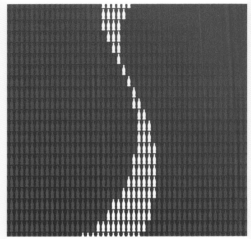

This "heart" graphic combines both icons: the contour bottle and the dynamic ribbon.

The new design had a far greater impact than anticipated. And, because consumers responded so well, the new design also helped loosen the internal culture at Coca-Cola by endorsing innovation more readily. It changed how employees viewed their brand and opened doors for people to innovate within the company. The new packaging design elements—that dynamic white ribbon backed by a little bit of yellow—unleashed the energy native to the brand. "Good design did not reinvent the brand but rejuvenated it," Gobé points out. "It released the latent potential within its image, its audience, and its company. The emotional energy of the brand was brought to life."

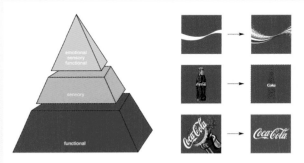

A pyramid chart demonstrates the progression of brand attributes and their different graphic manifestations (right), from functional (head) to sensory (heart) to emotional (gut), which incorporates both functional and sensory attributes.

The Coca-Cola club cans are slim and stylish, featuring craftmanship-like renditions of the signature contour bottle and dynamic-ribbon designs to cater to a younger and hipper crowd.

DASSAULT FALCON

Dassault is a company known around the globe for its leadership within the aviation and aerospace industries. For more than fifty years it has provided the world with the finest military fighter jets, engineering technologies, and military surveillance aircraft. Since the 1970s, the company has extended its unparalleled expertise into the realm of civilian aircrafts through its business jet division, Dassault Falcon, manufacturing the best-built business jets in the sky.

Desgrippes Gobé's partnership with Dassault Falcon began in 2001. Since then, the passion and intensity of the emotional brand experience has echoed the passion, intensity, and commitment to excellence of this world leader in aviation. Desgrippes Gobé began by redesigning their corporate identity and repositioning the naming of the company's signature jet, the Falcon 7X. The team then extended its emotional brand vision by utilizing the Internet to create Dassault Falcon's corporate website, Private Customer Portal, and a number of micro-site extensions such as the 7X Launch Site.

Branding the Flight Experience

The corporate identity Desgrippes Gobé created for Dassault could have been traditional and formal, emphasizing only the serious business aspects of owning a jet, but instead the imagery reveals the company's heart and soul, its passion for flight, and its commitment to design and engineering excellence.

Logging onto Dassault Falcon's website, the first images one sees depict the utter beauty of the company's jets, caught in photographs mid-motion as they glide through the sky. The images are truly breathtaking, giving a sense of the craftsmanship, innovation, and performance capability of these awe-inspiring "products." Desgrippes Gobé's mission was to fulfill the vision of Marcel Dassault, founder of Dassault Aviation, which centered around the proposition "for an airplane to fly right, it must be beautiful." This was a vision that only emotionally in-tune partners could truly understand.

The website is a tour through Dassault's past and stands as a testament to its stature and achievement as well as to its passion and vision in aircraft design. It also provides the latest information and tools to help discerning visitors in the initial stages of research, providing online tools that offer real-time information related to the operations of the aircraft. It is this fascination with and undying passion for aviation that comes through the website design and that is infused throughout the new corporate identity.

A More Human Identity

The slogan "Engineered with passion," displayed prominently on the corporate website, immediately calls visitors' attention to Dassault Falcon's main emotional message. The black background, vibrant emerald green accent color, and typography tipped at an aerodynamic slant all serve to strengthen and energize the message. The black also acts like the velvet interior of a jewelry box, making the photographic images pop for added drama. "The resulting design is a very humanized yet aspirational, emotionally charged presentation of the ultimate dream of flight," says Anneliza Humlen, account director for the project.

Part of Desgrippes Gobé's brand work was dedicated to leading the charge in bolstering awareness of the company's customer service division, a unique asset in the aviation industry that provides technical assistance and information 24/7 for Dassault Falcon customers. The Desgrippes Gobé team also helped develop and market programs and services under a newly conceived expression of "Customer Care" that led to the creation of a humanized identity system and strategy for the Dassault Falcon Customer Service Division. From the design of the aircraft down to the design of the corporate identity and website, the essence of Dassault Falcon is seamlessly conveyed—a perfect marriage of technical ingenuity and ingenious design.

The new corporate website for Dassault Falcon communicates the company's new positioning statement, "Engineered with Passion," to express the brand's vitality as well as its heritage. Combining shades of emerald green with black, the design team infuses the Dassault identity with weight, power, and emotion.

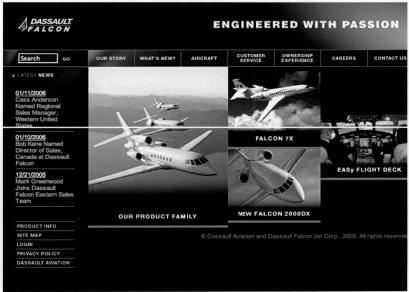

Desgrippes Gobé positioned Dassault's Falcon 7X business jet with its own launch site emphasizing speed and cutting-edge jet technology.

"Our challenge was to take that which is regarded as the ultimate in premium luxuries, the business jet, and use design and tone of voice to underscore the emotional soul of the Falcon Jet, which is its smartness and sexiness."

—Marc Gobé

The website not only details Dassault's many accomplishments and innovations, but also reveals the company's heart and soul, its shared passion for flight, and its commitment to design and engineering excellence.

DOMTAR

Package design can transform a seemingly mundane product into a colorful, fun object; in fact, more often than not, this is precisely the aim of the brand designer. Domtar, a global paper company, wanted to expand upon its friendly personality and brand story—expressed in the slogan, "Paper would be boring without people"—in order to stand out among other paper manufacturers in the market and especially on the shelf. Desgrippes Gobé came in to reestablish the Domtar brand identity and help it get seen and heard by creating lively packaging that communicated Domtar's unique brand voice. "Our goal was to bring the brand promise to life through illustration," says Wendy Gold, account director for strategy on the project.

People Paper

Consumers who are used to seeing dull pictures of office objects or uninspiring designs on their paper packaging are delighted to find people in Domtar's quirky silhouettes. In crisp white on different vibrant backgrounds, the silhouettes alternate depending on paper type. They capture everyday moments at the office with a twist—such as a man browsing through a file cabinet that balances a flower pot, a woman at the photocopier with a dog seated at her heels, a man typing at his computer next to his robot desk toy, a woman leaning back to toss a wad of paper into the trashcan (which also becomes part of the packaging layout), and more. These situations and gestures are familiar, and they are also comforting. They introduce the human element into the packaging, transforming what could be boring, blank pages into a friendly product.

"The people silhouettes illustrate a lifestyle of interaction between people and paper and convey individual personalities through paper usage," explains Gold, who collaborated with Phyllis Aragaki, account director for design on the project. Some of the packaging incorporates photographs of a cup of coffee, a mouse on a mouse pad, a close-up shot of a desk divider. "The photographs reflect both home and business settings, while another distinct aspect of Domtar's

personality—its brand voice—is communicated in the packaging design using various quotes, which act as a call to action with the product as well as add a level of humor and irreverence." The quotes not only give you something to read while waiting for a document to print—making the experience as well as the product enjoyable—but also convey Domtar's unique personality, as though it were another officemate waiting with you to use the printer.

From Commodity to Personality

Domtar's strong focus on the human element is completely unique among paper producers and resonates with employees, merchants, printers, and consumers alike. On the practical side, the design presents a clear system of color, type, illustrations, and icons that allows consumers to select a desired product quickly. Meanwhile, the humanistic design, with its familiarity, style, and humor, simultaneously builds awareness and distinction for the brand as a world-class personality standing out in a category filled with commodity products.

Some of the packagings incorporate photographs of familiar home-office and business elements, such as stacks of binders and folders, a stapler, and of course a cup of coffee.

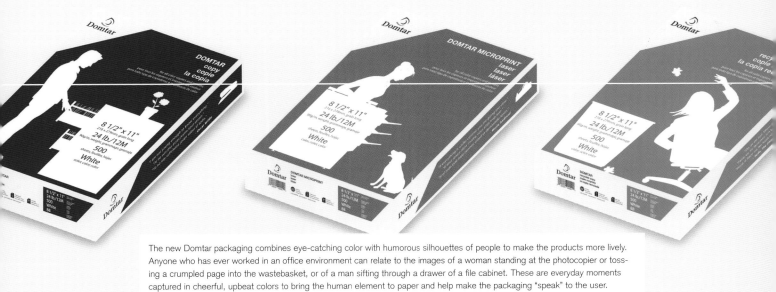

The new Domtar packaging combines eye-catching color with humorous silhouettes of people to make the products more lively. Anyone who has ever worked in an office environment can relate to the images of a woman standing at the photocopier or tossing a crumpled page into the wastebasket, or of a man sifting through a drawer of a file cabinet. These are everyday moments captured in cheerful, upbeat colors to bring the human element to paper and help make the packaging "speak" to the user.

"Paper would be boring without people."

—Domtar communication

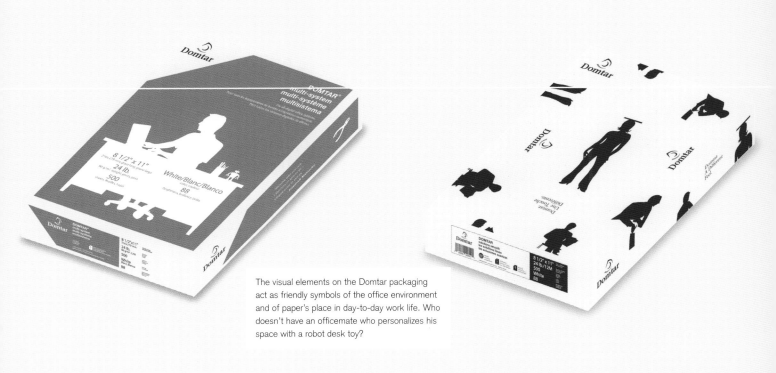

The visual elements on the Domtar packaging act as friendly symbols of the office environment and of paper's place in day-to-day work life. Who doesn't have an officemate who personalizes his space with a robot desk toy?

EFD PRINCESS PLUS DIAMONDS

Even premium luxury items, such as the incomparable Princess Plus diamond offered by EFD, need the help of a good brand designer. The Israeli diamond-jewelry manufacturer and De Beers partnership wanted to develop a brand presence in Japan for the Princess Plus, a dazzlingly cool square-shape "princess-cut" diamond that had previously enjoyed successful market campaigns in both the United States and China. EFD commissioned Desgrippes Gobé to prepare the Princess Plus for its Japanese market entry and to develop the initial brand strategy that would extend into the creative design concept as well as the booth design and marketing materials for the 2005 International Jewelry Trade Show in Tokyo.

Square Beauty

In Japan, as in the United States and China, princess-cut diamonds have become an alternative and particularly intriguing jewelry choice. The image of the square diamond is more about beauty, fashion, style, and luxury than about love or eternity. It breaks away from the traditional, classic cuts of centuries past and makes a timeless gem even more timeless, reviving and extending its unique presence into the future by attracting a younger generation.

The poster and brochure Desgrippes Gobé designed for the Japanese launch featured a young, independent woman who asserts her strong personality by determinedly testing something new on her tongue. She is not the passive, compliant type; instead this lady wants to try things out for herself. With her raised chin and defiant toss of her hair, she emits the saucy essence of noncompliance that the Desgrippes Gobé team wanted to convey for the brand.

The image also implies the particular, surprising "taste" of the Princess Plus diamond—sweet and luxurious, like a sugar cube. The experience of this new diamond is precious in many ways, but the real surprise is in the square shape, which is something many people have never seen or even conceived of in a diamond before. Who knew diamonds

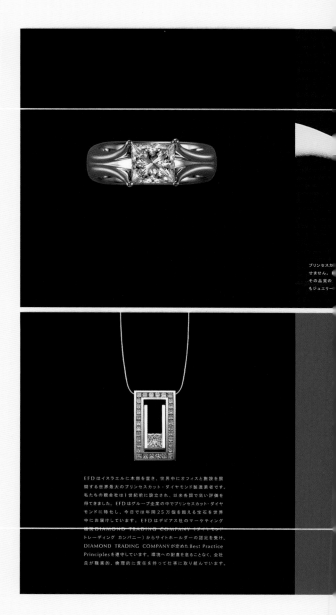

プリンセスカ
せません。
その品質の
もジュエリー

EFDはイスラエルに本部を置き、世界中にオフィスと施設を展
開する世界最大のプリンセスカット・ダイヤモンド製造業者です。
私たちの親会社は1世紀前に設立され、以来各国で高い評価を
得てきました。EFDはグループ企業の中でプリンセスカット・ダイヤ
モンドに特化し、今日では年間25万個を超える宝石を世界
中にお届けしています。EFDはデビアス社のマーケティング
機関DIAMOND TRADING COMPANY (ダイヤモンド
トレーディング カンパニー) からサイトホールダーの認定を受け、
DIAMOND TRADING COMPANYが定めたBest Practice
Principlesを遵守しています。環境への配慮を怠ることなく、全社
員が職業的、倫理的に責任を持って仕事に取り組んでいます。

EFD JEWELRY

えに難易度の高いカットです。高品質な宝石づくりには高度な技術と経験、蓄積されたノウハウが欠か
ットの世界最大のサプライヤーです。ヨーロッパの権威あるブランドのプロダクトにも採用されるなど、
これお客様がご存知なのです。また、私たちはプリンセスカットの魅力を最も知る立場から、自ら
けています。スタイリッシュでエレガントなTale of a Princess コレクションにご注目ください。

THE BEAUTY OF THE SQUARE

他の誰よりも輝くために、人はダイヤモンドを身につけます。しかしそのきらめきも、このオーラを前にしてはかすんでしまうか
せん。圧倒的な存在感を持って光彩を放つ、スクエア型のダイヤモンド。世に溢れたラウンドカットとは明らかに違うそのかたち
ブリリアンス。それは誰にも似ていない、何にも迎合しない、世界にひとつの個性をきらめく星のごとく輝かせます。スクエアは自己主張
エアは自分らしくありたいと願う女性たちの新しいシンボル。四角い石、それは強い意志にも似て…。いまダイヤは四角形へ、視

SIGHTHOLDER
DIAMOND TRADING COMPANY

"The EFD brand expression revolves around the
concept of opening your mind to new ways of
looking at the world. It shows how the objects you
thought would always stay the same can change
and transform and take on new features. It's an
exciting world to live in."

—Yoko Margaret Iwasaki, Creative Strategist, Desgrippes Gobé Tokyo

could come in shapes other than round? Who knew there were more cuts to make? What an invention, and what fun to explore the possibilities.

At the same time, the overall look of the advertisement retains a classic air: it is black and white, and the woman wears what appears to be a simple black dress and no other jewelry. However, this is a younger woman than we are used to associating with luxuries like diamonds. These subtle elements communicate that the Princess Plus is hip, young, and cutting edge—definitely cutting edge.

Desgrippes Gobé carried this last very important quality into the booth design for the EFD display at the 2005 International Jewelry Trade Show in Tokyo. By bathing the booth in dim blue lighting, the diamonds radiated a light all their own, which made a lasting, and certainly glittering, impression on visitors.

"The EFD brand expression revolves around the concept of opening your mind to new ways of looking at the world," says Yoko Margaret Iwasaki, the project's creative strategist at the Desgrippes Gobé Tokyo office. "It shows how the objects you thought would always stay the same can change and transform and take on new features. It's an exciting world to live in."

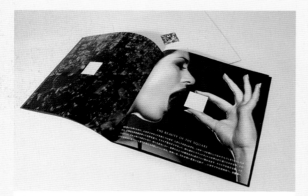

Marketing materials center around the image of an independent and decidedly hip young woman placing the Princess Plus square on her tongue. The toss of her hair indicates that she is not the passive, compliant type, and the overall image conveys the essence of noncompliance that the Desgrippes Gobé team wanted to convey for the brand.

Desgrippes Gobé created the booth design for the EFD display at the 2005 International Jewelry Trade Show in Tokyo. Dimming the lighting in the booth and infusing it with a sultry blue, the display dazzled visitors with the pure glitter of the diamonds themselves. The iconic image of a defiant woman putting a Princess Plus shape in her mouth is reiterated throughout, reinforcing the brand message of exploding convention.

ダイヤは、視覚形へ。
誰にも似てない四角いきらめき、プリンセスカット・ダイヤモンド。

◆E◆F◆D◆

EASTERN MOUNTAIN SPORTS

Brands live out of doors just as much as they live on store shelves. But before Eastern Mountain Sports (EMS) worked with Desgrippes Gobé, it did not view itself as a brand—it was simply a camping and sporting-goods store. EMS didn't have the aspiration or credibility to put its own logo on apparel or gear, thinking that no one would wear the store's clothing brand because it didn't stand for anything. Early on the brand's typical competitors were other mall-based, mom-and-pop stores.

Desgrippes Gobé broke new ground in research and brand-positioning strategy to give EMS not only a fresh vibe but also a wholly customer-focused business system. Expanding upon the emotional connection that outdoor enthusiasts have with nature and the gear that brings them closer to it, the team recreated EMS as a brand that met the demands of a vigorous lifestyle while not forgetting about family, friends, and, most of all, having fun.

Observation Is Key

Desgrippes Gobé determined brand initiatives by first auditing and diagnosing the retail environment, with the goal of achieving insights from actual customer behavior, not focus groups. They monitored customers' habits, needs, and day-to-day lifestyles to identify and prioritize opportunities where EMS could improve its performance. The key was to gain through observation a solid understanding of customers' beliefs, attitudes, and levels of knowledge.

In order to please the outdoor expert as well as the casual enthusiast, the Desgrippes Gobé team searched for a commonality that most customers shared, regardless of the degree to which they engaged in outdoor sports. "This was an eye-opening finding," says Peter Levine, creative strategist for the project. "Most consumers did not see the outdoors as simply the opposite of indoors. They felt that in fact indoors equaled something bad—manufactured spaces, fluorescent lighting, toxic materials, confining work cubicles—and that outdoors equaled not only good, but

The EMS logo captures the sense of outdoor energy and exploration with its dynamic tilt and vibrant green color. The initials stand strongly next to a steep mountain peak and rising sun, which form a directional pointing upward and outward from within.

the desired state of being, renewal, spirituality, and profound connection. It was imperative that we bring these emotions to life within the EMS identity and store experience."

The team used a variety of methods, ranging from "guerrilla research" tactics such as shadowing customers in stores to visual studies, video diaries, and interviews. The studies helped them to pilot "quick hit" brand trials in desirable demographic areas to evaluate the impact of different products and services on consumers' emotional experiences and to measure business results. These small-scale tests in turn fed into additional research and helped EMS prioritize its greater product and service implementation in a way that would drive an emotional connection with consumers.

"EMS wanted to make strong, personal connections with its customers," explains Marc Gobé, who with Peter Levine drove the design strategy for the project. "It wanted to speak their language, interact and engage with them in different life moments and contexts." Part of the strategy was to translate the company's early successes into consistent, sustainable business results. Desgrippes Gobé expanded upon EMS's valued offerings to create a consistent experience that began in the store itself and reached as far out into the world as the customer explored.

"Most consumers did not see the outdoors as simply the opposite of indoors. They felt that the indoors equaled something bad— manufactured spaces, fluorescent lighting, toxic materials, confining work cubicles. Conversely, the outdoors equaled not only good, but a desired state of being— renewal, spirituality, and profound connection. It was imperative that we bring these emotions to life within the EMS identity and store experience."

—Peter Levine, Creative Strategist, Desgrippes Gobé New York

A hat and T-shirt featuring the EMS logo carry the brand's identity outside the store environment. The logo is strong enough to stand on its own as labeling on all EMS wear.

Empowering Horizons

The imagery Desgrippes Gobé selected for EMS's overall visual identity captures moments of pure natural beauty earned after tough climbs and adventuresome wanderings. The pictures portray rocky peaks, clear vistas from mountain crests, thickly forested trails. The people who appear in them are obviously caught up in the moment, forgetting all their cares and communicating with the power of nature and exercise. Likewise, the images that don't include people speak through a human vantage point, revealing what it would be like to experience the moment oneself.

The slogans that accompany the photographs beckon with phrases like "Escape Your Reality," "This Way to Freedom," "Breathe," "Indulge Your Wanderlust." The visuals express the empowering experience one attains by pushing to the limit and getting out into the world, sharing life with family, friends, and nature itself. Desgrippes Gobé's ultimate goal in the brand's positioning was to empower customers in the store environment so that they feel they too can get out there and achieve their goals, in nature and in life.

The logo design harnesses the sense of triumph one feels after a hard climb or outdoor adventure. In a strong dark green, the initials form steep mountain peaks, so that the logo acts as a directional pointing to the sun, leading outward from within. The logo is powerful enough to stand on its own on jackets and other gear and brings the wisdom, passion, and know-how of the store staff to the forefront, which is critical to the expression of the brand's ultimate personality.

EMS products come with labeling that portrays outdoor adventures, placing the items, such as a backpack, water bottle, and gloves, in their right context. Labels and brochures were designed to inform customers about the products and their use.

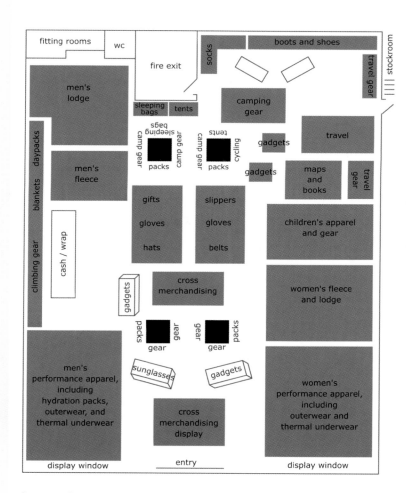

fitting rooms	wc		socks	boots and shoes

fire exit

men's lodge

camping gear

sleeping bags | tents

daypacks

blankets

climbing gear

men's fleece

cash / wrap

sleeping bags

camp gear — packs | camp gear

tents

camp gear — packs | cycling

gadgets

gadgets

travel

maps and books

travel gear

gifts

gloves

hats

slippers

gloves

belts

children's apparel and gear

gadgets

cross merchandising

women's fleece and lodge

packs

gear

gear

packs

men's performance apparel, including hydration packs, outerwear, and thermal underwear

sunglasses

gadgets

women's performance apparel, including outerwear and thermal underwear

cross merchandising display

travel gear

stockroom

display window | entry | display window

Desgrippes Gobé developed a store plan to make navigation as well as brand impact more customer-oriented.

ESTÉE LAUDER BEYOND PARADISE

In the past, Estée Lauder has been well established in the arena of refined, elegant, and luxurious feminine fragrances and beauty products that cater to women of a certain upscale but attainable lifestyle. The brand's unparalleled leadership in this market segment helped it to dominate in the United States. However, the refined and elegant approach did not make Estée Lauder a leader in Europe, where top brands project a more sensual and sophisticated attitude and wrap themselves in more dreamlike imagery.

Desgrippes Gobé, itself a company that bridges American and European styles, tastes, and temperaments, took on the brand design of Estée Lauder's newest fragrance, Beyond Paradise, with the goal of overturning perceptions of the brand and launching Estée Lauder into the higher echelons of the top global fragrances.

Beyond Real: The Making of a Fantasy

The brand narrative created for Beyond Paradise by Estée Lauder's marketing and design teams radiated from a fantasy realm of unending beauty and magic, a place you could escape to without going far, a dreamlike world just over the rainbow. Desgrippes Gobé was brought in to work with the Estée Lauder group to design and position the fragrance as a dazzling emissary from paradise, carried preciously in a dewdrop-shaped bottle made of rainbow-hued crystal. By using the fragrance, or by simply holding it in your hand, you could transport yourself to this magical place of sensuality and fantasy.

Desgrippes Gobé heightened the emotional energy behind the brand by conveying a message of free-spiritedness and optimism, inviting young as well as middle-age women to partake in a world of sensuality. The message taps into every woman's primeval draw toward make-believe and splendor, kindling images of lush gardens filled with exotic flowers and fragrances that never fade.

Beyond Paradise would widen Estée Lauder's audience base to include women from age twenty to forty-five, a younger age group overall than the brand usually spoke to. "The Beyond Paradise woman expresses the true spirit of Estée Lauder," explains creative strategist Peter Levine. "She is feminine and sensual, energetic and expressive, open and outgoing, generous and self-assured, free and optimistic. She is imaginative and young at heart, but not naïve. She is a woman who follows her dreams."

The Perfect Raindrop

Just looking at the Beyond Paradise packaging design is like catching a glimpse of a rare, fantastical world. You can almost taste the excitement the design team felt in creating the elegant, elongated raindrop, with its perfectly poised, liquid curves. The lines are simple and fluid, suggesting purity and lusciousness, its prismatic colors changing magically with each variation in light. The bottle looks good enough to drink. And this is just the point: a fragrance comes to life in all senses, not just the sense of smell; it connects with your sense of sight, taste, and touch. It connects with your imagination. The design conjures an exotic experience, like sipping dewdrops from flower petals in a mystical garden, while at the same time conveying a modern crispness and practicality; the bottle is designed to fit perfectly in the palm of your hand. The outer box design also fuses a magical experience of discovery with wonder in the natural beauty that surrounds us every day.

"Estée Lauder brought out what everyone thought was impossible: new luxury beauty products comparable with any European brand. It paved the way for America's entry in the global luxury business. Estée Lauder went where nobody expected it to go, or dared to go."

—Marc Gobé

Secondary packaging echoes the subtle rainbow shades of the bottle on the exterior, while the interior surprises with a bright coral-colored flower, evoking the floral scent waiting to escape.

The Beyond Paradise bottle combines imagination with simplicity to create an object of beauty. The lines are fluid, suggesting a raindrop whose prismatic colors change magically with the lighting. Even the cap is made of glass, extending the water theme.

Up and Away

In the past, Estée Lauder fragrances were rooted firmly in reality, expressed through more everyday images of brides, a woman walking her dog through a field of flowers, and other real-life moments. Beyond Paradise represents a major departure for Estée Lauder, away from a woman's lifestyle and into the realm of her fantasies, with a positioning that is distinctively youthful.

"Estée Lauder, once a purely mature 'status' brand, is combining status with a 'freedom'-brand mentality as it strives to reach a more international customer base and compete with the European brands," says Marc Gobé.

Patrick Bousquet-Chavanne, president of the Lauder, MAC, and designer fragrance division, emphasized that Beyond Paradise was "talking to consumers in a different way to get them to visualize the Lauder brand in a new place." It became a top-ten global fragrance soon after its rollout in early 2004, redefining Estée Lauder while revolutionizing the world market.

Preliminary bottle designs for the Beyond Paradise men's fragrance (opposite) play with the shape as well as colors of the original feminine version (above) to home in on a more masculine form that is still youthful and fantasy-based.

EVIAN

The History of Water

In the past, water consumption in the United States consisted of running the tap or buying bulky gallon jugs at the supermarket. It wasn't until the seventies that bottles of purified water imported from Europe began to appear in upscale restaurants, offering a sophisticated alternative to alcoholic beverages as well as an opportunity for Americans to relive their past romantic escapades to France, Italy, or the Alps. At the same time, models and celebrities were bringing the habit back from Europe to trend-setting locales such as New York, Los Angeles, and Miami. In the 1980s, a flood of new bottled waters went hand in hand with the health craze that took the American market by storm, providing more expensive but certainly more fitness-conscious waters for consumption at health clubs, the new social scene. Convenience-sized PET bottles facilitated hydration during exercise, and soon running shoes and water bottles became the badges of the true "achiever." The water brand you chose to drink became a statement about who you were.

By the late ninties, due to growing concerns about the deteriorating quality of municipal water supplies, a heightened awareness of healthful benefits from hydrating throughout the day, and a culture that was becoming increasingly more mobile, bottled water became a mainstream beverage. These days, it would be impossible to walk into any small-town grocery or step up to a street-corner vending machine without coming face to face with a slew of bottled water choices.

The one brand that has from the beginning claimed absolute iconicity in the category is Evian, as the most authentic, upscale water brand. However, with the proliferation of competing brands in the late nineties as well as growing commodification in the market due to beverage giants distributing processed municipal water, Evian was forced to revitalize its brand and reestablish its premium status. This was where Desgrippes Gobé came in.

Summitting the Alps

As one of the first bottled waters to enter the United States, by 2001 Evian had enjoyed a decades-long relationship with

the U.S. and world markets. An iconic brand, it embodied the very concept of bottled water to the American consumer. This, combined with its elite European heritage, proprietary presence at all the best bars, clubs, and restaurants in the hippest cities, and certainly its premium price and sleek bottle design, had kept Evian at the top of the pyramid as more and more brands became available. The single most important attribute of any water, of course, is its source, and Evian "summitted" them all, from the tips of some of the highest mountains in the world, the Alps. The label's familiar white-capped trio of Alpine peaks reinforced the brand's origins each and every time a consumer reached for an Evian bottle. The Alps, the label dictated, were the epitome of crisp, fresh mountain air, and its water the essence of purity.

What could compete with that? But as water makers from all over the world poured into the market, Evian had to confront brands such as Fiji, which distanced itself through breakthrough package design and bottle shape, and Vittel, which exuded a modern, youthful, and well-synchronized lifestyle approach in its package design and marketing communications, among many, many others. In order to reaffirm itself as the original bottled water, Evian had to transcend the concept of "purity" as well as capture the imaginations and loyalty of the health-minded youth generation.

Desgrippe Gobé's objective was to create an emotional "desire" for Evian beyond the consumer's rational "need" to drink water. The design team set out to fashion a brand image so uniquely Evian that it would be unassailable by any other brand. The challenge was how to re-infuse the brand with the energy and excitement it had when first introduced in the United States. The mission, in other words, was to re-create the "buzz" of the original brand presence.

The one-liter Evian bottle design brings a new ergonomic and sporty feeling to the old design.

Flooding New Territory

The design team conducted audits of international water brands, which were expanding rapidly and dramatically into new geographical and demographical territories. Mass-distribution players and other new market entrants, such as vitamin water, threatened to commoditize, even outshine, premium bottled water brands. The team analyzed competing brands, looking at both the various package-design innovations as well as each water's placement on a brand territory map created for the category. The map depicted a crossroads of four crucial territories, or attributes: functional, accessible, emotional, and original. In the late nineties, Evian had operated somewhere between the functional and original territories. The reintroduced Evian would cross the border into the land of the accessible and the emotional.

Desgrippes Gobé analyzed the different elements of the Evian brand in terms of the stories each element told. The product story was about its purity, its Alpine origins, its freshness, and French sophistication. This was also its "head" story, which aimed to meet people's rational needs through communications expressions. The lifestyle story talked about Evian in its hip, trendy environments, at fashionable nightclubs, in supermodels' kitchens, toted around by young, international urbanites. Here Evian's heart attributes thrived, cradled in a twenty-first-century lifestyle of better living, global interaction, and youthful style. Finally, Evian's emotional story spoke to the gut, to people's need for spiritual purity and health, to tap into the source and to be reborn. This story was about nature, the body, and personal radiance, the future of living itself.

Desgrippes Gobé delineated the target audience: customers ages fifteen to thirty-four, with a focus on fifteen- to twenty-four-year-olds. This audience was outgoing, technologically savvy, and image- and trend-conscious. The core user base also attracted those customers in fringe age groups, both the youth that aspired to the sophistication of older ages and the thirty-somethings who aspired to a youthful outlook. Through the SENSE® program, the Desgrippes Gobé team zeroed in on the brand qualities valued most by this target audience—image qualities of stylishness and sophistication and product qualities of purity and freshness flowing from the French Alps. These equities were then funneled into the brand platform and the corresponding imagery was created for the new identity, including new communications expressions.

> "Evian did not have to prove it was the best bottled water in the world—it was."
>
> —Marc Gobé

Evian Speaks

"Evian did not have to prove it was the best bottled water in the world—it was it," explains Marc Gobé. And this had everything to do with the personality the brand communicated. "It had to speak in the voice of one of the world's great brands: confident, relaxed, assured; charming and sophisticated; playful, fun, flirtatious; a bit bold, a bit unusual, and always fresh and original."

Product communications emphasized attributes such as "pure", "clean", "natural", and "refreshing", and these were invoked by the color palette and graphics of the new bottle design. Evian distinguished itself as a water with style and sophistication, traits that were part of its core identity.

The Look of Drinkability

The redesign for the one-liter Evian bottle merges the familiar label, snow-covered Alps included, and recognizable clear-plastic shape with an exciting new feel. The bottle shape has been carved like an ice sculpture, cool, contemporary, and unmistakably chic. The water's origins are stylishly outlined around the bottle's upper portion, while the bottom half zips and twists with modern, abstract lines in ski-track patterns. The design met the needs for a comfortable bottle with flair, elegance, and increased drinkability while keeping within strict manufacturing and budget constraints.

Designs for the new Evian bottle structure centered around ease of grip as well as a more sensory feel.

FAUCHON

The new Fauchon store in Paris provides an emotional invitation impossible to turn down. Devoted to delighting the senses, the completely renovated space has been transformed into a temple to the purely pleasurable, to emotion in the absence of reason. It is in a place, like Fauchon, where any craving can be satisfied by an unparalleled sensorial experience.

Desgrippes Gobé's task was to redefine the total brand territory of the famed fine-food store and to reestablish its historic flagship presence on the Place de la Madeleine in the city's fashionable eighth *arrondissement*. Through a revitalized store concept and visual identity, Desgrippes Gobé repositioned the Fauchon brand in its original luxury environment and transformed the store itself into a definitively contemporary theater of gourmet emotion, where taste and pleasure mix with exceptional quality, and where the products themselves are the stars.

Black and White, Pink and Gold

Photographs of the original Fauchon grocery stand, installed on the Place de la Madeleine by Auguste Félix Fauchon in 1886, depict a sense of old-fashioned quality and refinement. Here was the best fresh produce hand-selected by one of Paris's preeminent gourmand grocers. Desgrippes Gobé translated this essence into the elegant black-and-white letterforms of the new brandmark and then juxtaposed this authoritative pairing with vibrant magenta and luxurious gold to infuse the brand message with warmth, passion, and an air of culinary excellence.

Mainly white, the store owns a chic, airy feel. Nothing is placed too close together, so each product has its space to shine. A leisurely yet anticipatory atmosphere is created through the appointment of delicate hanging lamps, shimmering gold pillars, and sinuous stretches of display cases illuminated from within. Black gives power and a contemporary gleam to the floor and built-in shelving. Pink ignites sensuality and a bit of impertinence, spicing up wall spaces, lampshades, a curved stairway, and, most seductively, the recessed lighting in counters and wall

displays, giving the room an appetizing glow as well as a touch of glamour. Tempting hints of gold glimmer from shelf interiors and along sharp, graphic edges, while golden shopping baskets add just the right amount of indulgence to the experience.

One of Many, Many of One

The space is both fluid and powerful. Designing simple, modern furnishings with streamlined, black-and-white lines, the Desgrippes Gobé team wanted to valorize specific crafts and products by presenting them in their own specialty areas, which were designated for fruits, breads, pastries, prepared foods, caviar, wine and spirits, and more. "In each area, the merchandising is based on an interplay of the singular item versus the bunch, which sets a pace in the store and creates visual separations to highlight the exceptional amidst the generous, abundant offerings," explains Alain Doré, the mastermind behind the store's design concept.

This notion of the one versus the many, of selecting one delicious item to enjoy or deciding to purchase a handful or more to take home, is reminiscent of the traditional grocer's cart as well as a positively transcendent design idea. Reflected in the repeated "Fauchon" word background used to pattern the store awning, packaging, and advertisements, the notion of generosity and abundance is echoed throughout. Rows and rows of pastries alongside bundles of fresh produce, neat towers of caviar, swirling shelves of fruit (the core Fauchon product) all play into the larger visual composition, while each individual piece, set aside, is equally a delight to behold.

Food for the Senses

Peering through the large picture windows of the store's street-level façade, each one framed in thick black and an electric pink lining, one looks upon another universe—one in which the gourmand reigns supreme and countless new food presentations are produced alongside reinventions of

Each element has its place, with space to breathe. In an open corner, inset black shelves display colorfully packaged Fauchon goods.

"Fauchon is an ambassador of taste, an architect of desire—a veritable theater of gourmet emotion."

—Alain Doré, Creative Director, Desgrippes Gobé Paris

timeless classics. The silver spiral shelves spilling over with exotic fruits are, at the same time, a fantastically innovative way to display a product and a nod to the days of Fauchon's grocery cart. Smaller items are arranged in separate baskets made to look like old-fashioned paper cones and printed with the revamped Fauchon word pattern. The baskets line the display cases in a simultaneously orderly and disorderly fashion, capturing the intersection of the old and the new, the authentic and the visionary. Elegant black built-in shelves display multicolored packaged goods as well as Fauchon's world-renown wine selection.

In fact, the store itself is one delectable packaging system, incorporating crisp lines with the warm, seductive glows of pink and gold and distinguishing the high-end nature of the products on display. Everything glows with its own sublime light while blending with the space as a whole. As though inside a modern white jewelry box, the products—mouthwatering fruits, handcrafted chocolates, fresh pastries and breads, and delicacies selected from top sources around the world—twinkle like jewels themselves. Desgrippes Gobé's creation asserts Fauchon's primacy within the art of fine-food preparation and its particularly French savoir-faire. Most of all, it devotes itself utterly to the pleasure of the senses—all of them at once.

A billboard announcing the opening of the new Fauchon store on the Place de la Madeleine in Paris radiates the identifying colors of magenta pink, black, and white. The idea of exquisite, gourmet taste mixed with high fashion and glamour is conveyed through sensuous, glittering pink lips literally "eating" the signature white-on-black Fauchon motif of the storefront awning. The store's classic picture windows glow with dazzling displays of the delicacies found inside.

Touches of gold and hidden magenta lighting ignite the chic white interior of shop. The glossy black floors convey an utterly contemporary attitude, and inventive presentations of foods and packages are spread evenly along the counter spaces to give the whole a sense of air and delicacy. There is room to browse and to stroll along the perimeter, admiring the offerings on display.

Suspended from the high ceilings are delicate, old-fashioned glass lamps illuminating the display cases from above. Desgrippes Gobé invented a modern rendition of the grocer's cart fruit display in the far corner: silver spiral shelves spilling over with exotic, colorful fruits. The ceilings are given a high gloss to reflect the abundant light from the windows and hanging lamps, brightening the space.

A magenta stairway evokes today's fashion world, while black-and-white images of the original Fauchon grocery cart, placed on the Place de la Madeleine in 1886, add a sense of French history and tradition. Gold leaf has been used to paint the edge of the stair railing and a rounded column, heightening the gourmet atmosphere.

Through a sidewalk picture window, passersby can take in the plentiful rows of delicacies, conveying a sense of abundance while also emphasizing that one perfect piece to take home.

Bringing in another element of the grocer's cart experience from a century earlier, fresh produce is displayed in baskets made to look like old-fashioned paper cones printed with the Fauchon word pattern.

FRAGONARD

Brands often travel long distances to bring a taste of a different part of the world to people who live nowhere near it. The trick is to pack enough of the culture into the brand so that the taste is just as fresh, just as evocative as it was when it left its country of origin. For Fragonard, Desgrippes Gobé wanted to lift the perfume brand out of its localized reach and induct it into the international realm of quality fragrances and body-care products. The brand's regional origins in sun-drenched Provence, in southern France, would only help in the endeavor by certifying the authenticity of Fragonard products and providing them with a distinctive brand story.

An artisan perfumer for generations, the Fragonard brand symbolized knowledge in the extraction of Provençal flower oils and in the countryside's natural resources and materials. Desgrippes Gobé's objective was to valorize the brand's specific and genuinely French knowledge by giving it a contemporary expression. The team developed a total strategy that was both emotive and selective, defining first a revitalized brand territory and visual identity, including logo, and from there the vibrant personalities of the product lines, including the iconic Soleil de Fragonard fragrance, symbolic of the brand.

The Beauty of the Old in the New

In creating the Fragonard brand territory, Desgrippes Gobé rehabilitated the traditional perfumery bottle, which was historically used to protect the formulas from the damaging light and intense heat of Provence. This concept fed into the creation of a full range of eau de toilette fragrances, differentiated by color selections and packaging designs in harmony with the character of each scent, from fruit to floral, Oriental spice to au natural. Each fragrance comes in the traditional metal bottles from the past yet with modernized labeling.

For Fragonard's visual identity, Desgrippes Gobé wanted to capture the Provençal aesthetic, its unique way of life, by creating a brand expression centered around the sun. To do this they tapped into the perfumer's strong roots in sunny Provence, where purple lavender grows alongside roses and jasmine in the summer, producing valleys of vibrant color. The aesthetic beauty of this countryside is reiterated in the multicolored fabrics and scented products so particular to the region and known throughout France and the world.

The sun logo the team designed embodies both the prestige of the Fragonard heritage and the radiant qualities it brings along wherever it travels, infusing each new product creation with a connection to Provence.

"The Fragonard visual identity conveys a rich culture and regional reputation that is also international and refined in stature," explains Joël Desgrippes. "It says this is a perfume maker that is simultaneously selective, known among perfumers around the world, as well as utterly fresh and contemporary. It also tells the story of a region known among perfumers worldwide, a city that Catherine de Medicis unveiled to the world of perfumery through its industry of perfumed leather gloves."

All of the design expressions Desgrippes Gobé created for the brand validate the pure forms and materials used in traditional perfume making. Old-fashioned ways are evoked, through the hand pumps provided with the perfume bottles, while warm colors and gestural nature motifs convey Provence's incomparable colors, aromas, and climate.

Soleil de Fragonard

Desgrippes Gobé designed an iconic perfume to establish the brand on the international market. The Soleil de Fragonard fragrance shines with a completely unique handmade bottle structure and sun-shaped gold cap. Made with thick, mottled glass, the design is reminiscent of both tradition and luxury. From scent to color to packaging, Soleil conveys the matchless golden light of Provence and its particular Mediterranean-baroque accent. Desgrippes Gobé later introduced Grain de Soleil, a lighter fragrance with a rosé tint.

Extending the brand into the world of modern ambiance, Desgrippes Gobé defined Fragonard's aromatherapy product line, drawing upon an array of light floral scents. The brand also expanded into all-natural body-care products and more contemporary eau de toilettes, as well as a men's line.

"Fragonard is a brand that is lively and rich, constantly evolving," affirms Desgrippes. Designing with respect for the brand's essential characteristics, Desgrippes Gobé created a brand life for Fragonard that both valorizes and pays homage to its origins.

The curved bottle shape of the Eau d'Oreiller glows with a soft-gold tint reminiscent of Fragonard's sunny south of France origins. The sun logo, conveyed gesturally, adds a touch of the artisanal to the design, while the attachable hand pump reinforces the brand's origins in France's rich tradition of perfume making. A cloth sack serves as the brand's unique secondary packaging.

The Eau Fantasque bottle design retains the curves and golden tints of the signature Soleil de Fragonard while communicating a more classic, refined air with its rectangular red label and smooth bottle cap.

"The Fragonard visual identity conveys a rich culture and regional reputation that is also international and refined in stature. It says this is a perfume maker that is simultaneously selective, known among perfumers around the world, as well as utterly fresh and contemporary."

—Joël Desgrippes

Packaging for Fragonard products upholds the high quality of its origins by borrowing elements from the past, such as a woven cloth bag, the classic oval shape of a soap bar, and a simply designed silver bucket candle. The sun logo becomes both star and flower in these designs, hand-drawn to communicate Fragonard's brand story.

The bottle for the brand's signature fragrance, Soleil de Fragonard, has been rendered in roughly hewn glass, reminiscent of a time past, topped by a golden cap shaped like the Fragonard sun logo. The script on the face of the bottle is lively and carefree, evocative of the brand's southern country culture.

GILLETTE

With the success of the Sensor razor, Gillette was ready to extend its brand into the men's "grooming" category. This meant building a new line of products tailored to meet all of the shaving and grooming needs of the modern-day man. At the same time, the new line would send a message of providing the best technology in the category. Such a message is conveyed most effectively through a focused emotional design concept, making the project a perfect task for Desgrippes Gobé. The firm came onboard to develop the proprietary packaging structures and graphics for the new Gillette products, which would be launched simultaneously in Europe and the United States.

Made-of-Steel Design

Desgrippes Gobé conducted a comprehensive audit and analysis of the global market for men's shaving products, in which Gillette was already a leader but where one always has to keep an eye out for the competition. The team developed a set of strategically driven designs that met the demands of Gillette's worldwide leadership position and built upon its brand equity while capitalizing on the company's reputation for quality and innovation.

Using as a foundation the brand's existing power elements, such as the colors blue and black, the stainless-steel look, and expertly designed ergonomic handle grips, Desgrippes Gobé generated a unique packaging system structurally designed to sit firmly in a man's hand. The sides of the after-shave conditioner and deodorant containers, for example, echo the grooved steel grip design of the Sensor razor handle, making the bottles easier to hold while also conveying a fresh, modern look. The graphics for the Gillette grooming series were likewise designed to communicate an image of cleanliness, masculinity, technology, and quality, while establishing the product as the leader in the world of men's grooming.

"What makes this packaging great is not that the shaving system, the handle, and blades look pretty—"pretty" is not a Gillette word—but that the shaver's handle sends a strong message of the best technology any man can get in the world of shaving," explains Marc Gobé. "Blades are small and unconvincing unless their efficiency is explained to you in detail." And that is exactly what the packaging for the new product line does: it conveys what is high-tech, innovative, and powerful about Gillette products through groundbreaking design.

Material, and Emotional, Revolution

The Desgrippes Gobé team proposed using an invention that was revolutionary at the time: a plastic material that could be finished to look like stainless steel. The material was critical to the products' function and design, as well as their powerful emotional impact. Not only did it provide a certain weight to give them heft and a quality feel, but it also brought the line together under a coherent, unifying message, one that demonstrates an exquisite attention to detail and expresses a robustness of spirit that inspires confidence in the user. "It was a completely new way to package grooming products in this category," praises Gobé. "And Gillette, a company that considers design to be the lifeblood of its business, found a way to help us do this project on time, on budget, and with the silver design we recommended."

Being open to the challenges of developing new materials as well as introducing other key innovations, such as a transparent container that showcases the clarity and purity of the product and an easy-to-use push-button dispensing system, was essential to the success and customer acceptance of Gillette's new grooming products. "Visuals communicate better than words and in the case of the Gillette razor, the handle is the messenger for the blade," Gobé adds. "But it is the packaging here that really sets the stage—a most glorified stage—for this innovative product. After all, the blades can only speak for themselves when you shave! It is no wonder that [Gillette is] now clearly the worldwide leader in the shaving category."

"Visuals communicate better than words, and in the case of the Gillette razor, the handle is the messenger for the blade. But it is the packaging here that really sets the stage—a most glorified stage—for this innovative product. After all, the blades can only speak for themselves when you shave!"

—Marc Gobé

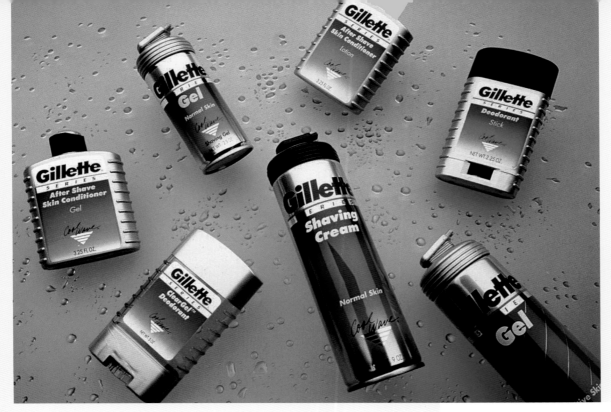

The design for Gillette's new line of men's grooming products drew from the brand's existing power elements, including the colors blue and black, the stainless-steel look, and ergonomic handle grips crafted to sit firmly in a man's hand. Graphics for the Gillette grooming series were likewise designed to communicate cleanliness, masculinity, technology, and quality.

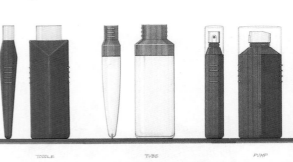

The invention of a plastic material made to look like stainless steel (shown here in a bottle cap) made the manufacturing of certain elements of the Gillette series possible. Beyond its functional role, the material also adds heft to the products to give them a higher-quality feel and unite them under a coherent visual and emotional expression.

The sides of the after-shave skin conditioner container echo the grooved steel grip design of the Sensor razor handle, making the bottles easier to hold while also conveying a fresh, modern look.

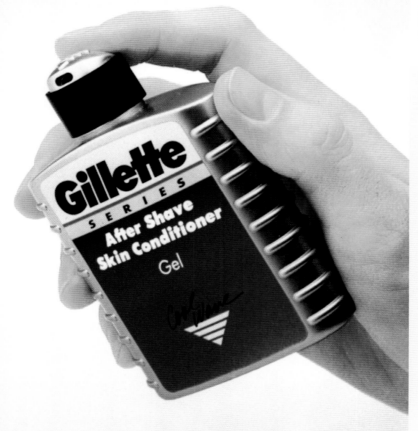

GODIVA

The particularly emotional relationship consumers have with chocolate made Desgrippes Gobé's commission to redesign the landmark Godiva store on Fifth Avenue in New York especially evocative of the firm's unique skills in emotional branding. The overall objective was to develop and implement a new retail strategy for the brand that would highlight Godiva's European heritage while also providing a more inviting atmosphere that encouraged browsing. In order to begin, Desgrippes Gobé went back to the "product"—essentially, indulgence—to reinvestigate the sensory experience people have with chocolate. And they had a lot of fun doing it; the office soon became saturated with chocolate's irresistible aroma as tasters poured in. "One of the most difficult parts of this project was keeping everyone from eating the samples!" laughs Marc Gobé.

It was just this experience the team had in the office that motivated them to apply the same sensory shift to the store itself and to recreate a place where the enjoyment of chocolate was paramount. Traditionally, Godiva stores conveyed an elitist message; decorated with black and gold packaging and heavy black light fixtures, they kept their chocolates tucked away and out of reach behind impersonal glass cases. Audits of existing stores revealed that shoppers found them too intimidating and thought to visit them only for special occasions. Though the brand's elitism helped to establish its original credibility, it had become too imposing to a younger, more experience-oriented generation that craved a little indulgence.

The SENSE® of Indulgence

Desgrippes Gobé proposed that Godiva use its SENSE® process to determine first the specific lifestyles of its existing and potential customers. When applied to Godiva, the SENSE® process exposed the fact that the brand's main audience—ranging from Baby Boomers, who, though focused on status, also demand rewards, to Gen X and Gen Y members, who are more attracted by experiences—was screaming for indulgence and sensuality. It discovered that the existing Godiva retail environment lacked the pleasure one feels with a chocolate experience, and that its relationship with customers was not focused on whetting their chocolate appetites.

Initial drawings for the Godiva store environment centered around the art nouveau aesthetic.

The new brand strategy was designed to retain Godiva's sense of elegance and luxury while losing the exclusivity and intimidation aspects. Positioning Godiva as "affordable luxury" heightened the brand as a chocolatier not only for special occasions but also for personal indulgence—a move critical to winning over the younger generations. Finally, an experiential link needed to be made between the sensuality of chocolate and the new retail design.

A Nouveau Look

Sometimes, for Desgrippes Gobé, it is during a visual audit, or the gathering of imagery for a project, that one strikes upon the unexpected and perfect solution to a design problem. This happened when Gobé was preparing for the Godiva presentation. "During a trip to Dusseldorf, Germany, a few weeks before the presentation," he recalls, "as I was walking down the street with one of our architects, we stumbled upon a fashion retail store that was designed in the art nouveau style, the same style that is so popular in Belgium, Godiva's country of origin. The style worked beautifully in this store, and we looked at each other thinking the same thought . . . this would be the perfect style for Godiva. Those luscious curves, which are so typical of the art nouveau look, seemed so appropriate for this project that we promised we would come back the next day to take some pictures. We almost didn't make it back to the store—in our excitement we had forgotten to note the address of the place—and it took us a couple of hours before we passed it totally by chance."

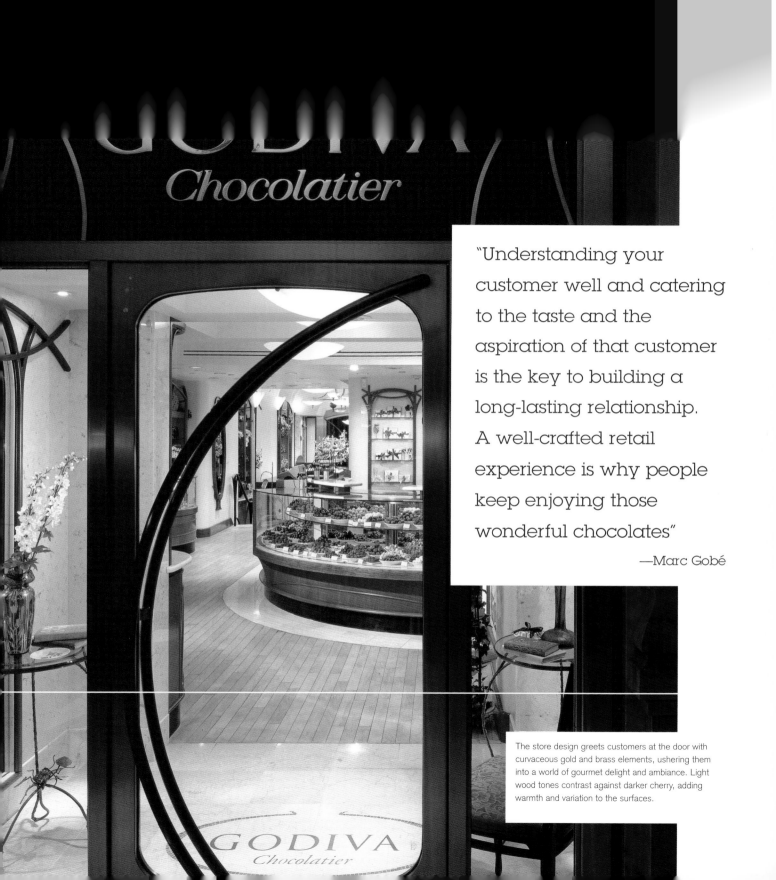

"Understanding your customer well and catering to the taste and the aspiration of that customer is the key to building a long-lasting relationship. A well-crafted retail experience is why people keep enjoying those wonderful chocolates"

—Marc Gobé

The store design greets customers at the door with curvaceous gold and brass elements, ushering them into a world of gourmet delight and ambiance. Light wood tones contrast against darker cherry, adding warmth and variation to the surfaces.

The Godiva management loved the idea, and the store design was put into motion. With the goal of expressing the intimate relationship a retail space must have with its customers, the design solution conveyed the sumptuousness of chocolate through the fluid, swirling lines of the fin-de-siècle art nouveau style, which incidentally emerged just twenty years before Godiva was founded in Brussels. The design stylized and simplified the art nouveau sensibility in the larger elements throughout the store, contrasting these with smaller, more detailed and eclectic fixtures. Self-serve merchandise was now showcased on cherry-wood counters, adding to the store's warmer feel. Prominent design features included counters and display tabletops made of white marble, a material traditionally used in making chocolate. A large, curved-glass case with two levels was specially designed to create a more appealing stage for the presentation of the unpackaged individual pieces of chocolate, while providing greater exchange between sales staff and customers.

As an added touch that delighted passersby, a chocolate-dipping station was placed by the store window, where the personnel would dip fruits into hot chocolate for visitors to taste, bringing a magical ritual into full view and encouraging more customers to enter.

The entrance to the flagship Godiva boutique on Madison Avenue in New York glows from within. The grandeur and elegance of the entryway represent the brand's origins in art nouveau Brussels and hint at the luxury and indulgence waiting inside.

Flagship Retail Design

The landmark status of the flagship boutique called for the unique structural elements, such as the vaulted ceilings, to remain intact. Desgrippes Gobé designed the retail environment around these important identifiers, enhancing them with custom fixtures, such as showcases and lighting, that were exclusive to the flagship store and would give the store its special atmosphere.

The finished design incorporated light wood tones contrasted against darker cherry, which added warmth and variation to the surfaces. Details such as the brass light fixtures, the graceful wall mural, and curved wire sign holders all contributed to the art nouveau aesthetic. The lush but refined style was also carried into the stemlike bend of the shop door handle, so that from the very first moment of contact with the store the customer feels as though she is stepping through time into an older world of European elegance and luxury.

"Understanding your customer well and catering to the taste and the aspiration of that customer is the key to building a long-lasting relationship," Gobé emphasizes. As a result of the new retail design, sales increased by 20 to 30 percent in comparison to the old stores, and the program was eventually rolled out worldwide.

In the shop interior, details such as brass light fixtures and curved wire sign holders contribute to the art nouveau aesthetic.

Shelving carved from dark cherry provides the perfect backdrop to the rich chocolate offerings. Art nouveau wall murals and the utterly unique gold inset ceiling add to the aura.

A cherry-based curved-glass case with two levels, designed exclusively for the store, creates an appealing stage for the presentation of individual chocolate pieces.

LES GRANDS MONTETS

Les Grands Montets is a veritable myth among expert skiers from around the world. Chamonix, the highest resort in France, offers some of the most difficult ski terrain on the planet. Desgrippes Gobé's task was to symbolize this exceptional site through the resort's image and signage systems and to conform the signage to the level of connoisseurship and security it provided. Desgrippes Gobé created a powerful brand identity that would ignite and uphold the common imagination of the international skiing community.

Pleasure and Danger Rolled into One

One reason why Les Grands Montets is such a mythic destination is because it offers technically challenging runs, with some of the steepest vertical drops of any ski resort, which are often covered in ice. The signage system designed by Desgrippes Gobé would help visitors maximize their enjoyment of the sport and get the most out of the extraordinary landscape. To do this, the notice boards are conceived as guideposts pointing skiers in the right direction while also warning them of upcoming dangers.

Desgrippes Gobé's design objective was dual: first and foremost to guarantee the safety of skiers by providing the necessary degree-of-difficulty information in an eye-catching, easy-to-read manner, and to support newcomers at lower levels who want to experience the myth for themselves. The signs would escort skiers down the slopes, advising them much like a high-mountain guide, attending to their needs as well as cheering them on, in winter as well as in summer.

The design solution balances the graphic codes signalling the theme of high-level performance with a more natural, reassuring aesthetic. Desgrippes Gobé generated a specific pictorial language to accompany skiers on their adventures. Using triangular shapes to express dangers and rounder forms to convey pleasure, the pictures set in place a kind of traffic law for the resort. All color codes and graphics are designed to be easily understood, leaving no room for doubt as a skier speeds down a run, where decisions have to be made in the instant.

"We developed a powerful, high contrast symbology, making the oppositions especially strong, and the imagery direct and exaggerated, so that the information would go straight to the skier's brain. Every sign was thought through to maximize the comfort and safety of the skiers," says Joël Desgrippes and Alain Doré, who headed the project. The idea was to allow skiers to anticipate and activate their reflexes and to get the right information at the right time for the best ski experience in one of the most beautiful high-mountain settings in the world.

What's in a Sign?

Les Grands Montets' signage system was thought through carefully and objectively to maximize the efficiency of information conveyed and inspire confidence in skiers' hearts and minds. This leaves the performance up to the skiers who come to share in the myth, freeing them to experience what Les Grands Montets has to offer. This is why the logo uses simple color coding to convey a crisp white peak and a star placed like a guide in a dark-blue sky.

The Grands Montets logo symbol appears boldly on signage outside a café area near the slopes.

The bold yet simplistic Grands Montets logo stands clearly out across all applications, including gondolas at the mountain.

Clear, distinct signage symbols present cautionary information for skiers setting out on the main lift.

The architects kept the building's original copper roof since, like the snow, it blends very well in this protected site.

point de vue	danger avalanches	télécabine	Piste bleue	restaurant
escale	danger chutes de glace	télésiège	piste noire	self-service
skis à la main				snack
se présenter par 3				téléphone
piéton				toilettes handicapés
sac à dos par terre	danger crevasses	téléski	piste rouge	snack
espace fumeurs	danger croisement	téléphérique	piste verte	bar

Signage for Les Grands Montets keeps to vibrant primary colors and black and white shapes so that it can be easily read by skiers racing down the slopes. The symbols range from warnings to markers for lifts, vista points, and where to get lunch.

"We developed a powerful, high-contrast symbology, making the oppositions especially strong and the imagery direct and exaggerated, so that the information would go straight to the skier's brain. Every sign was thought through to maximize the comfort and safety of the skiers."

—Joël Desgrippes and Alain Doré,
Creative Director, Desgrippes Gobé Paris

IMPERIA

In many cases, a name brand provides us with our only connection to a culture different from our own. Due to vodka's recent rise in demand, as more and more social drinkers in the United States and elsewhere opt for vodka as their drink of choice over any other liquor, vodka brands have exploded into new shapes, desires, and offerings. With its well-known Russian origins, vodka continues to play its authenticity card, and those brands that opt to build their strategy on attributes relating to vodka's heritage always claim a strong standing among those offshoot brands that go the route of experimenting with naming and bottle design in order to distinguish themselves.

Imperia is one of those classic vodka brands that gives us a taste of the culture that made it. A trusted, premium vodka, Imperia represents the heritage and credibility of Russia's national beverage. When it hired Desgrippes Gobé to reposition the brand, including its naming strategy, bottle structure, and graphics, Imperia got the chance to revitalize its old-fashioned look and feel as well as launch a design that links back to its cherished Russian origins.

Tradition with Modernity Stirred In

With so many new vodka brands pouring into the marketplace, the category is expanding in size to accommodate vodkas that suit every mood and situation. Like Smirnoff and Stolichnaya, Imperia counted itself among the elite inner circle of authentic brands and so wanted to make a powerful new statement about itself in order to affirm its standing.

"Voluntarily or involuntarily, you can find a vodka that matches any of your emotional needs," says Marc Gobé. "In a business where taste is irrelevant and where one product cannot realistically compare itself to another, the emotional positioning is all the brand has to stand out in the marketplace. When there is little in terms of taste differentiation, brands must revolutionize their presence in order to convince consumers that they can enjoy a product that they might think of as generic."

Desgrippes Gobé delineated three brand "pillars" for Imperia that establish its characteristics in terms of customer, product, and attitude. The brand's customer is a style-conscious, discerning, and urban social drinker; the product itself is "premium," clearly about authenticity, a modern classic with its own distinctive allure; and its attitude has "badge status" as an original Russian brand, which communicates

The Imperia silhouette makes an elegant, luminous display behind the bar.

"Instead of caving into the monopoly of one brand style, the vodka category has expanded along emotional promises that allow every brand the opportunity to succeed by connecting with people's various desires."

—Marc Gobé

The faceted glass of the bottle structure evokes the Russian love of classic ornamentation, while the clean simplicity of the translucent design communicates Imperia's purity of distillation and ranking among the world's premium vodka brands.

primal passion, power, and sexiness that is distinctively Russian. To create the visual positioning, the design team gathered imagery of typical Russian objects and icons, as well as visual clips of cool design, and blended them together, fashioning a new bottle and label graphics.

Standing Proud

The name Imperia captures the royal status of the brand while making it more memorable on the shelf, where vodka labels crammed with Cyrillic letters can be confusing to browsers. The typography retains the Russian feel, using the iconic color red to match the red cap, as well as black and silver to make the wording pop. Another aspect of the graphics, designed by Tom Davidson, is that the words run up the sides of the bottle—an innovative style of labeling that readily catches a buyer's attention.

When it came to the new bottle design, the team narrowed the overall inspiration down to two key elements: the importance of the original design, with its distinctive flair at the bottom, in terms of brand recognition and loyalty, and the image of a proud Russian man standing erect in a long fur coat and traditional tall hat. "We expanded upon the original shape, making it much taller to signify that this was a premium brand," explains lead designer Sam O'Donahue. "The cap is tall like the man's hat and an imperial Russian red. It also hides a cork, which is a surprise for the customer as well as one of the traits of a signature vodka brand."

The majestic stance of the Russian man, with his proud shoulders exuding love and pride for his country, provided the regal as well as human-like silhouette of the new bottle shape. The glass is faceted at sharp angles to evoke the country's admiration for classic ornamentation, refined and elegant, thus evoking a sense of heritage. At the same time, the design keeps its features clean and simple, communicating Imperia's premium status and purity of distillation.

The tall red "cap," strong "shoulders," sharply faceted body, and distinctive flair at the bottom of the new Imperia bottle structure convey the brand's heritage as well as its premium status. The label runs up the side of the bottle in Russian red lettering, distinguishing it from other brands on the shelf.

Initial designs played with the royal-red color and beveled body shape.

JOHNNIE WALKER APPAREL

From whiskey label to designer label? Why not? With the loyal following the Johnnie Walker brand has amassed over the years as the world's first global whiskey, it wasn't difficult for the name to expand into a new category. Desgrippes Gobé came on to reposition the Johnnie Walker apparel line through an innovative "shop-in-shop" concept. A brand that has been around as long as Johnnie needed an excuse to slip out and talk to the young folks. By situating its apparel line around its whiskey sales it could entice a younger generation to interact with the brand and boost Johnnie Walker shares in the whiskey market.

The Traveler Brand

The shop-in-shop concept speaks directly to the target customer's interests while at the same time expressing the brand's core attributes, which spin off its founding-father presence as a whiskey brand. Twenty-five to forty years old, the Johnnie Walker customer loves to travel and is somewhat sophisticated, affluent, and masculine in an understated way. The original Johnnie Walker logo picturing a striding man worked perfectly as the symbol for the apparel line. The image inspired the travel theme Desgrippes Gobé worked with to design the shop interior, a space that celebrates the spirit of adventure and establishes Johnnie Walker as a global brand in tune with its loyal patrons' values and interests.

A Total Life Experience

"The brand positioning placed Johnnie Walker at the forefront of a new wave in marketing that places products within total life experiences, not the other way around," says Marc Gobé. "The product becomes part of something larger and more meaningful, a lifestyle the customer has an emotional investment in." The apparel line allows Johnnie Walker customers to sip their favorite whiskey while wearing the outfit that fits the mood and the context. The store design communicates the brand's masculinity and

Communicating masculinity and refinement, the store design incorporates wood and metal elements for a clean and modern feel, catering to a young and progressive audience. Time-zone clocks set to the actual time of the featured destination line the walls, and a wall-mounted flat screen plays videos and soundtracks that convey the brand's travel theme.

"The brand positioning put Johnnie Walker at the forefront of a new wave in marketing that places products within total life experiences, not the other way around. The product becomes part of something larger and more meaningful, a lifestyle the customer has an emotional investment in."

—Marc Gobé

refinement, with textures that are modern and clean but rich at the same time. And, while visually evoking the brand's Scottish heritage, it also maintains a young and progressive overall feeling.

To reinforce the travel theme, a back-lit screen features seasonal travel destinations that are relevant to the Johnnie Walker customer. Time-zone clocks are used in conjunction with the signage and set to the actual time of the featured destination. A wall-mounted flat screen plays videos and soundtracks that echo Johnnie Walker's brand positioning.

Minimal, elegant steel components help fixtures contrast with the wood slating, adding a touch of sophistication and modernity to the entire environment. Overall, the colors and materials exude a masculine elegance that blends seamlessly with the environment and allows for seasonal presentations.

The final design caters to the brand's traditional customers but is versatile enough to reach a younger audience. Travel becomes the point of entry into the world of the brand and its products, from whiskey to apparel for older customers and from apparel to whiskey for the new youth generation.

A back-lit screen built to look like a picture window features seasonal travel destinations relevant to Johnnie Walker's adventurous yet sophisticated clientele.

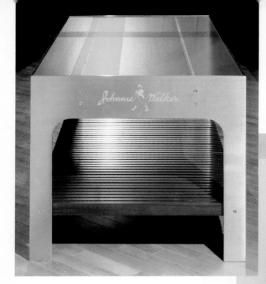

Minimalist steel components like this shelving unit provide an elegant contrast to the wood textures. A stainless-steel suitcase adds a thematic touch to the corner, presenting the clothing—mainly sports jackets and trousers suitable for a sophisticated traveler—in their right context.

Unique shelving components designed for the Johnnie Walker store epitomize masculinity. Here, a square, steel frame is juxtaposed with wood slotting.

Labeling hints cleverly at the brand's Scottish heritage with a classic Scotch plaid background, against which the recognizable striding man emblem and logo script are posed.

JOHNSON & JOHNSON SOOTHING NATURALS

Johnson's Baby is a brand steeped with such emotional power and a rich heritage, in many ways it serves as the face of Johnson & Johnson to consumers around the world. As the number-one maker of hair and skin-care products for babies, Johnson's Baby puts their users first, developing high-quality, timeless, and trusted products. The company makes a commitment to providing users with the most advanced developments in the skin-care field, and recent strides in moisturizing lotions and shampoos have given Johnson's the opportunity to offer customers products in their natural skin care line, Soothing Naturals. These new products offer a perfect blend of clinically tested formulas and Johnson's endorsed ingredients. Desgrippes Gobé was brought in to conceive a visual identity and graphic language that would properly express the special attributes of this new and natural opportunity for Johnson's Baby.

New Ingredients, New Presence

Johnson's Baby launched its newest addition to the family in late 2005. As project manager Anneliza Humlen explains, "[Desgrippes Gobé's program] was about reinterpretation of design equities and sensorial cues to achieve new opportunities of communication and balance for this much-beloved brand. The challenge, as with all launches, was to communicate the freshness of the Soothing Naturals product while stretching and evolving Johnson & Johnson's existing brand equities."

The design team created a new yet complimentary graphic language of soft, clean hues to create a balance between the line's ingredient-innovation story and the emotional strength of the Johnson & Johnson heritage. It designed the logo to look confident and natural next to the Johnson & Johnson brandmark. The subtle sage green of the script, reiterated in the bottle caps, infuses the design with a look that speaks to the products' quality ingredients. These ingredients, which make up the core attributes of the Soothing Naturals lotions and shampoos—pure vitamin E, olive-leaf extract, and skin-essential minerals—are symbolized by the olive-leaf visual topped by a pleasing baby-blue water drop.

For the design of the bottles themselves, Desgrippes Gobé focused on pure, harmonious structural shapes to communicate an equal interest between baby and mom. The bottles themselves come in shades of cream and white, adding depth to the cooler greens and blues of the graphics as well as reflecting those colors commonly found in nature. The team also utilized the surface finish and details on the packaging to express premium and thoughtful elements that suggest an added touch of care within a mass-market environment.

A Design for the Generations

The Johnson's Soothing Naturals packaging design perfectly conveys the unmatched quality of the exclusive formulas they contain. The solution is a natural extension of the market's leading franchise, long an icon and well-loved by generation after generation of mothers and their children. The visual vocabulary Desgrippes Gobé developed provides a platform from which future Soothing Naturals line introductions can grow.

"Johnson and Johnson Baby products have a strong emotional connection with consumers. With that connection came very specific expectations, both in product presentation, and performance. That said, we needed to evolve consumers' perception of the brand and get permission to take it further. That's what Soothing Naturals did."

–Judd Harner, President, Desgrippes Gobé New York

The refreshed graphic language of softer, clean hues introduces subtle sage green for the Soothing Naturals logo script, reiterated in the bottle caps, which speaks to the products' quality ingredients. Rounded, harmonious bottle shapes with specially crafted surfaces to make them smooth to the touch cater to both baby and mom, while the bottle colors of pale green, pink, and cream echo those colors commonly found in a baby's room. The Soothing Naturals logo of the olive leaf and round water drop crystallizes the line's all-natural positioning.

KENZO JUNGLE

Knowing the client's personality and being able to craft a narrative that brings this personality to life are the key components in beauty branding. In building the visual territory for the fragrances in the Kenzo Jungle series, the Desgrippes Gobé team drew its inspiration from Kenzo's fashion collections and especially from long conversations with Kenzo Takada himself. Each fragrance expresses a distinctive facet of the charismatic designer's imaginative world. The colorful, luxurious, and vibrant traits that personify Kenzo's collections and are true to his personality inspired the team. The addition of the elephant on the bottle's cap has become the brand's iconic feature, suggesting its most distinctive and intimate values.

For the sake of consistency in creating the Jungle series, Desgrippes Gobé embarked on the invention of a compelling narrative for the brand. What "story" would the Kenzo Jungle fragrance tell? What images would it conjure, what mood would it evoke? By integrating all elements of the design, from scent to packaging to brand narrative, Desgrippes Gobé aimed to communicate the essence of both the Paris-based fashion designer's colorful, vibrant personality and his aesthetic vision, self-described as exotic, luxurious, surprising, and sensual. The design also marked a shift in Kenzo's visual expression from vegetation-based motifs to those inspired by wildlife.

A Perfume for Each Season

By creating seasonal perfumes that would tie back to Kenzo's fashion collections, Desgrippes Gobé's global strategy was to establish a connection between the world of perfume and the world of fashion. As fashion rules that collections change and evolve according to the seasons, the design team applied the same concept. Just as a fashion accessory reflects the personality of the person who wears it, the bottle caps were conceived as accessories that customize the individual scents. In this way, Kenzo pioneered the concept of seasonal perfume, and the Jungle bottle design and packaging have initiated a new trend that today is followed by many other brands.

Paramount to the project's success was the fact that Joël Desgrippes knew Kenzo very well, as he personally knows all the people for whom he builds brand narratives. "I can't work for a creative person without knowing his or her intimate tastes," Joël insists. "With the Kenzo Jungle brand, I knew I had to emphasize the color and the animal nature of the brand narrative. It is very playful, and this is a part of Kenzo's personality. It has lots of color, it is very vibrant, it is very happy, and this also reflects Kenzo's personality. The elephant is Kenzo's good-luck charm."

Drawing the Urban Jungle

The initial two feminine Jungle fragrances implemented this strategy, one with a tiger-shaped cap and the other with a cap shaped like an elephant. The strategy was then to expand upon the design of the feminine versions to encompass a masculine scent represented by the zebra, Jungle pour Homme. Here again the imaginary Jungle narrative is a recurrent theme, handled with humor and combined with an urban narrative about the zebra in the city.

Sketches for the zebra-themed Jungle pour Homme men's fragrance bottle play with natural, dynamic curves as well as a square, masculine body. The cap is imagined as topped with a tuft of striped wild-boar's hair.

The initial bottle design for the Kenzo Jungle fragrance featured an elephant-shaped bottle cap to evoke an exotic brand story as well as the designer's playful personality. As an animal that means a lot to Kenzo personally, the elephant became the iconic figure for the brand.

"It can always be said that there is a Desgrippes Gobé design style, but more important, the object that we design reflects the personality that we created it for . . . We are the expression of the brands for whom we work. We melt away and are always very discreet in our work."

—Joël Desgrippes

The zebra stripes on the bottle are used as a symbol for the shadows and lights reflected in modern cities. The zebra-shaped cap recalls a masculine world but in a less literal, more symbolic way. This perfume feels like an invitation to travel back in time to the heart of the jungle while at the same time expressing an urban environment and the excitement of the city.

Each fragrance in the Jungle series is packaged in a box that folds out to create a miniature stage set for the animal featured. The backdrop expresses the distinctive personality of the scent while at the same time evoking the rhythms of Kenzo's fashion collections. Each season a new jungle animal is featured corresponding to a fresh scent and new color palette.

Every aspect of the final design communicates and emphasizes the Japanese background of the fashion designer. The clear, clean lines of the bottle contrast with the exoticism of the cap, which is cast in zamak, a soft, warm metal expressive of sensuality. Meanwhile, the foldout packaging introduces an element of play when opening the product.

The launch of the Kenzo Jungle global territory was the first to correlate the rhythms of fashion and perfume. By creating a perfume bottle for each season, Desgrippes Gobé's design has set a precedent in the perfume industry.

Aligned with the following fashion season, Kenzo introduced the tiger-shaped bottle cap for its second fragrance. Figured atop the pleasing glass-brick shape of the body, the caps are crafted from zamask, a soft, warm metal expressive of the romantic sensuality of each wild beast.

The Jungle Pour Homme bottle is bolder with a vertical, rectangular shape and slightly asymmetrical lines that maintain the clean, modern sophistication of the feminine fragrance designs. The added embossed zebra stripes give the flacon a grip, and the metallic cap topped with a tuft of real wild-boar's hair ties the product back to the Jungle series.

The packaging for the Jungle Pour Homme series echoes the zebra theme with embossed stripes, while the pistachio-green window behind the wordmark and lining the interior of the box infuse the entire package with energy.

The foldout packaging introduces an element of play when opening the product while strengthening the theme of the fragrance's color palette and providing an imaginative back-story.

LIME

At a time when media programming is rapidly expanding beyond television, media brands are claiming territory across multiple platforms in order to compete for presence and differentiation. When LIME, a health and well-being channel, launched its TV, Web, mobile, and radio presences in 2005, it not only introduced a twist to brand naming, it put a spin on the category itself. With the slogan, "Healthy living with a twist," LIME carves a new niche in lifestyle programming, treating a broad spectrum of topic areas generated by and for next-generation users.

Desgrippes Gobé came onboard to develop LIME's strategic platform, name, and visual language. This was more of a challenge because of the multitude of competing channels already taking up words like "health" and "well-being." The Desgrippes Gobé team decided to approach the problem from an emotional perspective. At the drawing board, the possibilities were endless, but with a little effort and more importantly with open minds, the name "LIME" was born.

What's in a Name?

"Naming is one of the most important parts of a branding strategy," says Marc Gobé. "Finding a new name is always difficult and challenging: Where do you start? Where do you find the inspiration and the relevance for a new name? And how do you find a name that is available?" The designers knew they had to think about the company from an emotional perspective that allowed them to think in metaphors, rather than a functional one which focused on how the company worked and what services it provided.

"LIME was not the direction one would expect, but emotionally it expresses freshness, bite, and purity," Gobé explains. "The meanings behind 'LIME' are active and transforming, an added positive element, a memorable, refreshing taste that gives a little kick to life. Emotionally it was right; the brand wanted to cover the transformative aspect of a balanced life as well as an active participation."

The name is transforming enough by itself to convey a unique, even revolutionary way of seeing one's health and future well-being. As creative director David Israel contends,

The LIME logo script is crisp and contemporary, with an inventive letter *i* whose dot has been twisted into the shape of a tiny lime.

A storyboard pasted along a sidewalk reflects the brand's hip, vibrant color combinations and eclectic style.

"There was an opportunity to lead the health and well-being media-programming category by redefining it. To date, the category has been defined by a consistent and clichéd style of naming and positioning. What no one had done was claim the next wave of the category."

—David Israel, Creative Director, Desgrippes Gobé New York

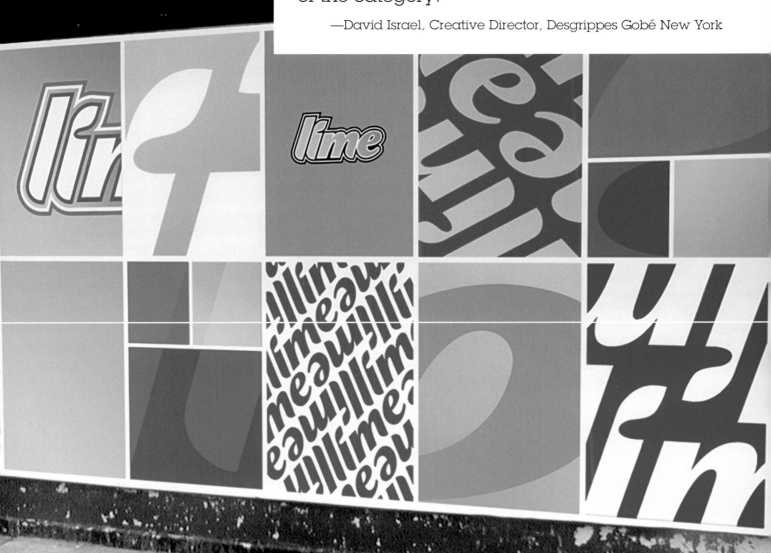

"There was an opportunity to lead the health and well-being media-programming category by redefining it. To date, the category has been defined by a consistent and clichéd style of naming and positioning. What no one had done was claim the next wave of the category. LIME is natural, fresh, bright, clean, and a little tart. LIME is the new green."

From Metaphor to Logo

Launched by Revolution Living, a company founded by Stephen M. Case, cofounder of AOL, LIME taps into emerging trends in both consumer behavior and media. "Healthy living is a trend that is becoming more mainstream," Case points out. "We can create a brand that unites a fragmented category. Second, the idea of building a next-generation network was intriguing to me." Log onto LIME's website (www.lime.com), where you can link to a potpourri of editorial, broadband video, and community content created by next-generation users, or tune in on your TV, mobile phone, or Sirius radio, and you will realize the genius behind the LIME concept.

Organized around topic areas—such as food, health, body and soul, fitness, people, and the planet—LIME caters to a new generation of people, who want a healthier, greener, more balanced lifestyle. "At its core, LIME is a resource that values opinions and community as well as inspires debate and reflection. To be entertained and yet be mindful of the choices we make in what we eat, how we live, what we buy, and what inspires us," explains Founder and CEO C. J. Kettler. "LIME isn't preachy, cliquey, or better than anyone— that's why our tag line is 'Healthy Living with a Twist.' You might go to yoga but have a cocktail afterward—we do our best a little at a time."

Playing off the emotional feel of the LIME metaphor it had created, Desgrippes Gobé worked on building a lasting logo shape—a satisfying wedge of LIME—and color palette—a zingy green—that were optimistic, fun, fresh, and welcoming without sacrificing credibility. The unconventional color combinations appeal to a younger, hip crowd. The brand imagery is energetic without being too peppy, fun without being light. It captures the freshness of LIME and, most important, its cutting-edge role in the world of lifestyle media brands.

The logo symbol of a refreshing wedge of lime with a witty slogan speaks to the unconventional attitude toward healthy-living programming the media group conveys. The green color is not only lime green but also hip and uplifting.

Advertising posters play off the lime shape, even transforming it into a retro TV set. The ads' quirky character expresses LIME's goal of providing a more down-to-earth and contemporary view of what healthy living is all about.

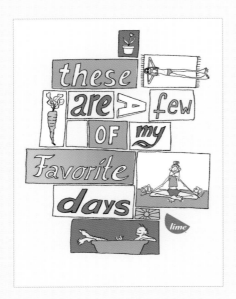

Posters with fun and unconventional cartoon figures and lettering cater to a new generation of viewers who might have only a passing interest in New Age lifestyles.

MUSASHINO UNIVERSITY, JAPAN

Often a design transcends a singular object or product and encompasses the entirety of an organization's brand universe, its inner and outer attributes as well as its global presence. Like a work of architecture, a brand design has more than two dimensions. It not only paints a cohesive, coordinated logo on the outside of the building, it also creates the mood of the interior, the feel of the building's furniture, the expression of its wallpaper, its cyber personality. This is the type of project Desgrippes Gobé took on for Musashino University in Japan, one of the country's oldest Buddhist universities. The challenge the design team faced was to help the university adapt to the complex social and educational environment of the twenty-first century. Due to the country's declining birthrate, Musashino is among the many educational institutions that are competing for a smaller student body and so need to bump up their branding design in order to attract future generations of students.

A Logo with a Human Touch

Desgrippes Gobé undertook a research and strategy program with key stakeholders in the university to create a brand concept that balanced the university's age-old Buddhist roots with its contemporary mission. This creative platform supported a renewed visual expression, presenting the university in a fresh and modern manner, with a dynamic new logo symbolizing the power of connection and progress. Desgrippes Gobé also created a brand statement, "Linking Thinking," to symbolize how Musashino University understands and actively supports the connections between people, ideas, and ways of living.

The statement perfectly describes what is communicated through the revitalized brand design. Desgrippes Gobé created the vibrant purple and white color palette and logo for the university. Since purple is a traditional Buddhist color, seen throughout the world in Buddhist temples, it affirms the school's strong Buddhist roots as well as breathes strength and authority into the visual identity. As shown on a student's T-shirt, the flower-like design looks

hand-painted, evoking both the symbolic Japanese cherry blossom and a student sketch of interconnected molecules, like bursts of thought, or fireworks in the sky. The gestural style is fundamental to Desgrippes Gobé's aesthetic belief system, since the firm is committed to making brands that are humanistic and that have a personable feel. The logo extends to the dynamic and colorful student credit card, stationery, and school-bus exterior, linking all of these elements into one cohesive and integrated design to express the school's motto of connection. The brand's digital presence is similarly conveyed through its website, which implements the same color palette, hand-painted logo, and "Linking Thinking" slogan.

On the credit card and stationery, the gestural drawing blends beautifully with the Japanese characters, reiterating the flower-blossom motif so integral to Japanese art. With a simple, handmade marking, the design brings to life the sense of discovery, exploration, artistic thinking, and human development that can take place only in an enriching educational environment.

Students model T-shirts in both purple and white on which the university's logo symbol is prominently displayed.

武蔵野大学
MUSASHINO UNIVERSITY

武蔵野大学は、新しいブランドマークと共に、
新しい歴史を拓きます。

武蔵野女子大学から武蔵野大学へ。2003年4月、私たちは新たな一歩を歩み始めました。また、2004年4月より
男女共学へ移行すると共に、初の理系学部である薬学部を新設（設置認可申請中）し、総合大学へと進化。
この校名変更と総合大学構想を機に、新しいブランドマークが誕生します。新しいブランドマークは武蔵野大学の
めざす教育の理念を示し、「目覚め」、「つながり」、さらにその「広がり」を表しています。武蔵野大学はこの新しい
ブランドマークと共に、人間教育を重視した建学の精神を受け継ぎながら、未来に向けて新しい歴史を拓きます。

武蔵野女子大学から 80年の歴史を背景に	▶	2004年4月	
		男女共学 （全学部）	薬学部 （設置認可申請中）

"If you look at a logo like this one for Musashino University, with purple flower designs that are reminiscent of a child's hand painting, and the whole visual language we create around it, what you see is a trademark that looks like it is hand-touched; it is more spontaneous, it is humanistic. That's the look and feel, the sensorial approach that has always transpired in our work. Whether we are in our work. Wherever, it is always consistent."

—Joël Desgrippes

A poster conveys the university's "Linking Thinking" slogan with simple, pared-down elements, including the deep-purple mascot color and gestural white flower motif.

Linking Thinking

A student credit card elegantly blends the gestural flower symbol with a rich purple background.

武蔵野大学
MUSASHINO UNIVERSITY

答えは、あなたの心のなかにある。

一人ひとりの生には大切な意味があり、何かを成すために、私たちは生きています。だからこそ、自分って何だろう、自分に何ができるのだろう、そう誰もが一度は自問し、自分と真剣に向き合おうと努力するのです。そこには、揺らぎ、戸惑い、焦りなど、いろいろな気持ちが交錯するでしょう。だけど、私たちはこう考えます。「答えは、あなたの心のなかにある」と。

私たちの新しいブランドマーク、それは「目覚め」"awakening"、「つながり」"link"、「ひろがり」"growth"の3つの要素を表しています。同時に、一人ひとりの心のなかにある生きることへの大切な意味が込められています。

自己に目覚め、個人と個人、考えと考え、ビジョンとビジョンがつながり、ネットワークが限りなく広がっていくこと。そこにこそ、次代を切り拓く力が宿っている。その信念のもと、私たちは、あなたの心のなかにある輝きを広い世界へと導いていきたい。 —Linking Thinking—

武蔵野大学
MUSASHINO UNIVERSITY

〒202-8585 東京都西東京市新町1-1-20
Telephone 0424-68-3142 Facsimile 0424-68-3322

Linking Thinking
www.musashino-wu.ac.jp

Inverting the purple ground and white lettering, this poster has a fresh, modern feel. The background incorporates suggestive imagery of concentric circles created in water, tying into the "Linking Thinking" theme.

A Musashino University catalogue pictures a low horizon and vast, purple-tinted sky, conveying the themes of intellectual exploration and discovery.

From Musashino University stationery and business card designs to signage for the university in a local train station to school buses, the identity remains lively, elegant, and eye-catching.

A website page for the university combines the purple mascot color and logo symbol with imagery, here a tree-lined alley that conveys tranquility, thoughtfulness, and intellectual exploration.

NATURA

A new beauty market has evolved, one in which a heightened world consciousness is valued higher than seduction. Today's youth generation is more interested in the welfare of the environment than in the welfare of their makeovers, and this is leading a trend in the marketplace centered around living in harmony with those around you.

Desgrippes Gobé Paris gave life to a complete brand strategy for the skincare-product and fragrance maker Natura based on the concept of respect for humans and nature as a means of attaining world harmony. From the definition of its brand territory to its design expressions, Desgrippes Gobé aligned every aspect of the Natura presence with the brand vision "Preserve and Respect," including identity, product design and line development, and communications tools.

The Elemental Language of Harmony

Desgrippes Gobé first developed a language for the brand that would express the harmony found in natural imperfection. The team crafted a design vocabulary that paired the attributes of authenticity and sustainability (through pure ingredients and sound technology) with those of diversity and humanity (through amorphous bottle shapes and natural imagery). It then defined brand pillars for each attribute: *authenticity*—integrity and lack of artifice, *emotion*—harmony within natural imperfection; *sensuality*—confidence, the human touch; earnest technology; *earth*—round and omnipresent, our DNA.

Taking the lush landscape of Brazil as inspiration, the designers explored four fundamental visual territories: the various wild imagery inspired by the three natural elements of vegetable, mineral, and water, and the warm, sensuous imagery stirred by the humanistic element of relationships, embodying the qualities of love, sensuality of touch, gesture, diversity, and universality. The earth-based elements provided subtle color tones and textures expressing nature and its essential qualities of purity, vitality,

Packaging for the Natura Humor antiperspirant offers humor and style, pairing black-on-white paper-doll doodles with energetic handwriting and a heart-shaped exclamation mark, to communicate the product's affinity with the playful side of romance. Package design by Gragnani.

"Brands exist through the power of their vision."

—François Caratgé, General Manager, Desgrippes Gobé Paris

and giving life. These were paired with more human elements to locate an emotional visual bond between the two.

"Looking close, you begin to see the sensual gestures a leaf makes, the emotional curves of a natural landscape," says Caratgé. "There is an essence in nature that corresponds to the human condition, to human emotions, and vice versa. This is the vision we wanted to capture in the Natura design. And this is important, because all brands exist through the power of their vision."

The Beauty of Imperfection

For Natura's skincare line, Chronos, every aspect of the design evokes a sense of natural purity and balance as well as imperfection. Bottle shapes are asymmetrical and more about fluid movement than perfect symmetry. The materials provide a milky-white sheen and frosted-glass translucence. Letterforms are light and supple, evoking the body and retracting from the spotlight. Every detail of the packaging suggests that the most important part of the product is found inside, in the all-natural, high-quality ingredients, not on the bottle's surface. "By unifying the cap with the body of the bottle in one reduced, imperfect form, the design communicates that it is about 'more product, less container', attained through better product technology," Caratgé explains.

The Natura perfume line extends the design vocabulary into individual bottle shapes and understated graphics. A perfect picture of nature, each bottle is a "unique" creation and complementary to the others. The designs are natural, elemental: appearing handcrafted, as though just off a potter's wheel, the bottle architecture for the Hoje, Sintonia, and Biografia scents comes in different imperfect shapes in moss-green, earth-brown, and water-blue shades, respectively.

For Humor, Natura's more alternative fragrance, the bottle design plays with primal sculptural figures, again much like the flawed yet beautiful shapes that surprise you in a pottery shop and that are deeply connected not only to a timeless human craft and tradition of natural elegance, but also to those fundamental minerals within the clay that formed them. Finally, for Natura's Plants line, Desgrippes Gobé fashioned bottles in elementary shapes that reflect the essence of simplicity.

Bottle shapes and packaging for the Natura Gem Fragrances rely on natural curves and colors, from earth-brown to off-white, to communicate their brand message.

The Natura Humor bottle shapes are primal and humanlike, in rich red tones that graphically express the theme of romance behind the fragrance.

The Chronos bottle designs convey a sense of natural purity and balance as well as imperfection. The lid to the moisturizing cream container dips in an asymmetrical but fluid movement. Milky-white and frosted-glass materials along with light and supple letterforms help the container glow from within.

The Atomos design pairs a rich-green cap with translucent green glass, simplifying the container to focus customers' attention on the contents. Finely stitched lines connect the two halves and are incorporated into the packaging as well.

PAYLESS

Payless is one of the world's largest specialty retailers, with more than 4,600 stores in the western hemisphere and an average of 600 million customer visits each year. Founded in 1956, the brand pioneered the self-service shoe store format and has owned the position of affordable family footwear for decades.

Anatomy of the Payless Brand Transformation

In 2005 a new leadership team arrived with a commitment to overhaul the brand.

It all started with a vision and a smart plan. CEO Matt Rubel came from Cole Haan, fresh from that brand's successful transformation. Payless worked to better understand the market, its broad customer base, and emerging opportunities. Research revealed that the existing consumer experience with Payless was rational—a decision based on price and convenience—but that there was little emotional bond with the brand. It also reinforced the fact that people love shoes! A tremendous amount of excitement and emotion surrounds the purchase of shoes, but this emotion did not transfer to Payless. Even Payless loyalists lacked an emotional connection with the brand.

The Payless team crafted a brand positioning that would tap into the rich emotional potential in its category and link it to the brand's equity in affordable footwear. To reach this goal, they drafted a new brand essence: "Inspiring Fun Fashion Possibilities for the Family . . . Payless." The team also did extensive work on brand personality. Importantly, the Payless leadership team simultaneously committed to improving its product. It increased its on-trend product collections and enhanced its designer collection and designer alliance strategy, which was a first in footwear.

Branding Partners

Payless hired Desgrippes Gobé to bring the brand to life by creating a new logo and accompanying visual identity system—a "look and feel" for the brand. At the same time, Payless hired the Seattle-based architecture firm Callison to design the new stores. While these were separate projects, the branding and architecture teams worked together closely to ensure a seamless brand transformation.

Desgrippes Gobé started with an immersion session that provided the brand history and gave an overview of the research and the new Payless strategy. In order to lay the groundwork for design, Desgrippes Gobé distilled the brand strategy into a streamlined set of attributes:

1. "Fresh and upbeat." The tone will be spirited and positive. Capitalizing on the positive emotion already associated with shoes, Payless seeks to be seen as a source of new styles that are both exciting in the store and even more exciting when they are a part of consumers' lives.

2. "Inspiring." A shift to more trend-conscious fashion will enhance the brand's image as a place for great ideas.

3. "Accessible." No longer accessible just in its pricing and ubiquity, Payless will be the provider of accessible fashion and fun.

4. "Savvy." Rather than being viewed as inexpensive, the brand will be seen as a smart purchase for shoppers in the know.

 "The brand is both inspired and inspiring. With great styles across targets, the possibilities really are endless," said Judd Harner, President and COO of Desgrippes Gobé.

The New Payless Logo

Though familiar and easily identifiable, the existing brand logo was dated and ran counter to the brand's desired image as a place for exciting, cutting-edge fashion. A new logo would signal a commitment to change, reinforce the new brand positioning, and present an exciting new Payless brand to the world.

With this brand strategy as a guide, Desgrippes Gobé embarked on an intensive design exploration. Designers were inspired by the idea of a kaleidoscope, which was by nature visually stimulating and provided endless combinations of color and form. As a kaleidoscope turns, the colors and shapes inside shift to form unique and interesting images. The new Payless logo introduces an icon for the brand

"A lot of companies meet with us and say that they want to re-imagine their brand. Many times the risks turn out to be too high to take that leap. Not Payless. When they said it, we knew they were dead serious."

–Judd Harner, President, Desgrippes Gobé New York

inspired by a kaleidoscope's shapes and sense of motion. The designers kept the Payless orange as a key color and as a nod to the brand's heritage, and embedded a letter P in the icon as well.

The designers also set out to modernize the Payless wordmark. The existing Payless logotype looked dated and out of style, and so they reached for a more contemporary look. Using modern rounded letters, they created a bolder and friendlier custom typeface.

The new identity shifted the emphasis on the brand name "Payless" and away from "Payless ShoeSource," as the brand was known in the past. The team thought of eliminating "ShoeSource" entirely, but consumer research signaled a disconnect. With a new logo, a change in brand name could cause confusion. In light of the broader identity changes, "ShoeSource" provided a necessary cue to the brand's past and allowed customers to understand that their brand was evolving within the new logo.

Not by Logo Alone: The Visual Language

A new logo can't do everything by itself. Once the new logo was approved, Desgrippes Gobé moved to the next stage and developed a supporting visual language. This is a virtual toolbox of elements that work together to create a branded "look and feel," including color palettes, type treatments, imagery styles, layouts, and other graphic considerations.

Payless has multiple targets, which presented unique challenges for the visual language. The brand needed a unified look and feel as well as distinct graphic treatments for the women's, men's, athletics, and kids' departments. Desgrippes Gobé created a look for the whole brand, as well as customized directions for designs that would speak to specific audiences. Kids' became more playful, women's more elegant and feminine, men's more subdued, and athletics bolder and more dynamic. As part of the visual language, Desgrippes Gobé created a number of graphic patterns that use the icon form in exciting, unexpected ways.

Desgrippes Gobé also created a logo launch video that premiered at the internal brand launch meetings. Additionally, the Desgrippes Gobé designers worked closely with Payless corporate communications to create the new business cards, stationery, presentation templates, and a whole host of Payless paraphernalia, including hats, banners, postcards, and water bottles.

Store Design

The entire store experience was significantly overhauled by the Callison team. Payless was known for its extremely tall racks of shoes arranged by size. Customers would have to venture down dark, cavernous aisles and peer into open shoeboxes in their size section to see what was available.

If Payless was going to be about "fun and fashion," the first major change had to impact product presentation. The Callison Architecture team dubbed the retail concept "Fashion Lab," and the organization committed itself to organizing the store by style, allowing the customer to explore and experience the trend and product "stories" curated by the brand.

Key branding elements were used throughout the store. The color palette was incorporated, which generated a friendlier, more fun, fresh, and upbeat environment. Shoe styles were grouped into "fashion stories." Real-life imagery of people enjoying their shoes was placed throughout the store. The Desgrippes Gobé team's visual patterns were also incorporated—from the textiles used in seating to promotional posters and window displays.

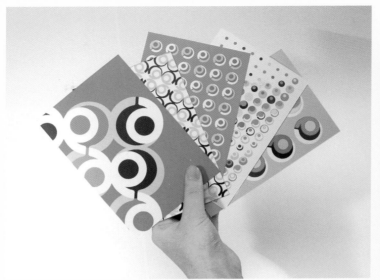

PELTIER

In 2003, Desgrippes Gobé Paris, in close collaboration with the Tokyo office, took on a commission from the confection distributor Juchheim Co., Ltd., to restage the Peltier brand in Japan. Peltier had become a tired and fragmented brand in urgent need of a revitalized graphic identity and a more dynamic and contemporary retail and product lines expression. Ultimately, the Peltier brand concept sought a deeper, more sensitive connection with its customers. Joël Desgrippes and his team of designers in Paris and Tokyo set out to elevate the brand cachet of Peltier in Japan, with its first challenge to build an exciting flagship store in Omotesando, the epicenter of luxury brands in Tokyo.

Haute Couture Food

After conducting a thorough brand audit and competitive review, Desgrippes Gobé first created a stylebook to outline Peltier's new image. This design step established an all-encompassing, innovative, and ownable territory for the brand. The book was called in French *L'éveil des sens, dans le respect du savoir-faire à la française,* or "The awakening of the senses through French *savoir-faire.*"

"I wanted to create a genuine emotional bond between the Peltier brand and the customer," explains Joël Desgrippes. "Like a maiden voyage in a sea of sensation, it will deeply awaken the senses. This is truly a fusion of French *savoir-faire* and Japanese sensitivity." The reinvigorated design aimed to stimulate all five senses, so Desgrippes collaborated with Philippe Conticini, the internationally renowned *patissier* in charge of Peltier's product development, to ensure a sensory feast.

The first step in crafting Peltier's new identity and brand expression involved revisiting the logo. Fresh typography was designed using classic yet modern forms, giving the name a timeless feel. The team fashioned the logo symbol by shaping a pastry chef's hat out of two conjoined Ps for Peltier, conveying a strong sense of Parisian elegance very much like that of the insignia over the doors of French craftsmen.

With classic yet modern typography and an insignia in the shape of a pastry chef's hat formed by two Ps—refined and playful at the same time—the Peltier logo conveys Parisian elegance with a contemporary edge.

The glass and steel façade of the Peltier flagship store in Omotesando, Tokyo's luxury-shopping center, is definitively contemporary in its design.

Color also played a vital role in the restaging, and the team selected three: a light saffron yellow to give brightness and life; a dark brown to reinforce the artisan and prestige attributes of Peltier; and a sweet, shimmery white to unify the light and dark tones of yellow and brown. These three "tasty" colors awaken the senses and generate an emotional connection between customers and the retail space. Inside the store, the colors play out in striking architectural details, such as the warm and welcoming saffron walls, the chocolate-brown wood floors, and white leather chairs and tabletops. The modern gleam of the stainless-steel counter streaks through the space, adding an exciting counterbalance to the more traditional elements of the design.

Package designs come in all shapes and sizes depending on the product. Chocolate and pastry boxes have clean, tapered corners like the crisp folds of a French napkin. The coloring reflects the rich, appetizing tones of the shop interior, in chocolate brown, caramel, and a sunny yellow.

"I wanted to create a genuine emotional bond between the Peltier brand and the consumer. Like a maiden voyage in a sea of sensation, it will deeply awaken the senses. This is truly a fusion of French *savoir-faire* and Japanese sensitivity."

—Joël Desgrippes

Packaging Peltier

The packaging was also revisited, since it is the crucial, expression of Peltier's rejuvenated food and gift items, including chocolates, cakes, and confections, that are purchased, transported, and enjoyed outside the store environment. The new package designs exude an undeniably contemporary sophistication and come in all sizes and formats depending on the product, making them excellent gifts in themselves. Metallic plates and canisters glow in soft yellow, pink, and caramel tones, while the chocolate and pastry boxes communicate with clean, tapered corners, much like the crisp folds of a French napkin or the expert scissor cut of a grand couturier. Each thoughtfully crafted package conveys the same visual message as the retail showcase.

But the ultimate achievement of the Desgrippes Gobé group was to conceive of an entirely new retail architecture for the prestigious Omotesando boutique in Tokyo. The strategy followed the thinking of the packaging: the space would be resolutely contemporary but cordial and comfortable at the same time. The floors were designed in a subtle dark-brown Wenge parquet so as not to distract from the items on display. Pearly white and yellow walls married with golden-bronze silk *kakemono* give the shop an air of precious refinement. Even the details of the sales counters, practical yet luminous, emphasize the products without distracting hungry eyes.

Craig Briggs, director of Desgrippe Gobé's Tokyo office, feels that the design fits well among the firm's many achievements in emotionally branded design. "From beverages to beauty, from luxury to mass [market], from technology to transportation, the power of emotion is a formidable tool to differentiate your brand from competing brands and to win over people's hearts," he says. Walking into the Peltier store, it is easy to see and feel why.

A Peltier storyboard evokes the brand's modern attitude and gourmet ingredients.

Desgrippes Gobé created a stylebook to outline the new Peltier image, establishing package designs and a color palette to describe the brand territory.

Peltier's insignia is found throughout the shop, including a plaque embedded in the shop floor.

The interior of the Peltier shop blends contemporary materials with dark brown parquet floors and warm yellow walls. A stainless-steel and glass counter gleams in the middle of the space, providing an exciting contrast to the more traditional elements.

Modern designs in crisp white leather offer alternative seating in the shop.

Restrooms continue the stylish contrast between dark wood and stainless steel.

The Peltier logo glows through the glass façade of the Omotesando shop at night.

Peltier packaging combines pale tones of caramel, pink, and rich brown suspended in a glowing white case.

RAKUTEN EAGLES

Fans dress themselves in Eagles jerseys and hats and use their bats to make noise.

All sports fans crave an icon they can rally around. Like the chosen team itself, a logo inspires camaraderie, community, loyalty, and provides fans with something they can hold up and say, "This is what I stand for." The logo becomes a visual expression for themselves, especially when they don team jerseys, caps, and color-coordinated outfits. For the Rakuten Eagles, Japan's first new baseball franchise in fifty years, Desgrippes Gobé wanted to capture the concept of multiple identity layers coming together, making new connections between what on the surface might seem like dissonant elements. Although baseball originated in the United States, it has extended around much of the globe and has become Japan's most popular sport. And as with many imported crafts, baseball ("ya-kyu") in Japan has modeled its own unique culture that, while sharing attributes with its American counterpart, carries its own distinct look and feel.

Go Logo!

Desgrippes Gobé designed the team's new uniform and cap, developing a fresh logo that would appear on all Rakuten Eagles expressions, along with a wide array of fan paraphernalia, including flags, pins, buttons, knit hats, jackets, and miniature bats. As most Japanese baseball teams have corporate sponsors, Rakuten is the name of Japan's largest online retailer. The Eagles differentiated themselves through their need for speed, since one of the main objectives was to field a young team whose primary virtue, and advantage, was speed on the field. An initial decision for Desgrippes Gobé to make, then, was how to express this vital part of the team's identity. From there, the logo took wing, featuring dynamic lettering that gives it the sense of dashing for home plate and even taking flight.

The "Eagles" logo name features an E and S that not only fan out on either end like a pair of wings but also emulate Japanese written characters. The Japanese-style E is repeated on the cap. A similar treatment was given to the players' numbers, giving the numerals an unmistakably

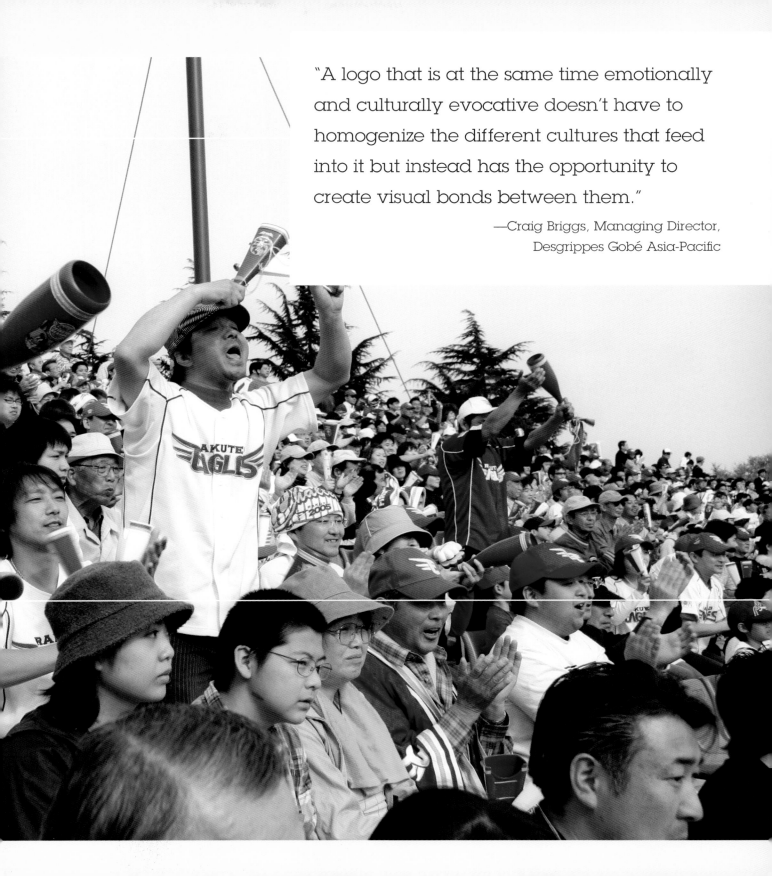

"A logo that is at the same time emotionally and culturally evocative doesn't have to homogenize the different cultures that feed into it but instead has the opportunity to create visual bonds between them."

—Craig Briggs, Managing Director,
Desgrippes Gobé Asia-Pacific

Japanese flair. The logo looks as though it will fly off the front of the jersey, while the unique blend of Eastern and Western features anchors it in its cultural identity: This is a Japanese baseball team, the logo says, while paying homage to the Western origins of the sport.

What is special about the new logo is that neither the Japanese identity nor the Western one disappears—both are present in the design. "A logo that is at the same time emotionally and culturally evocative doesn't have to homogenize the different cultures that feed into it but instead has the opportunity to create visual bonds between them," points out Craig Briggs, managing director. The design is a synergy of two cultures. Neither identity is lost in the mix.

A fan's mini baseball bat (above) and knit cap (below)

Team pins incorporate the winged Eagles logo.

With a dynamic winged logo, the Rakuten Eagles' cap and jersey communicate the number-one skill the team is known for: its speed on the playing field.

A giant Eagles cap crowns the entrance to the ballpark.

Eagles' mascots rev up the crowd and add a little humor to the game.

The uniforms combine American and Asian influences, integrating Japanese
lettering styles into the logo design along with classic Western features.

STARBUCKS SUPERMARKET PACKAGING

To point out that Starbucks coffee shops are on every street corner these days would be redundant. Everyone knows that the coffee purveyor has extended its stark green, white, and black emblem across the globe into cities both big and small. So when the company decided to expand outside its specialty-store environment and onto supermarket shelves, it needed a new graphic identity that not only announced itself to shoppers but also make sure not to sacrifice Starbucks' competitive points of difference. Desgrippes Gobé stepped in to create a visual identity for the packaging that was both coherent and allowed for the expression of vastly different coffee-blend personalities.

The Personality of Coffee

By the time Starbucks was ready to walk the grocery-store aisle, the company was importing beans from dozens of countries around the world ranging from the exotic to the more commonly visited. At the same time, it was creating its own specialty blends to suit its customers' individual lifestyles. In order to convey the breadth of choice a customer would have and to match a blend with that customer's particular tastes, the coffees needed to express through their packaging just what kind of atmosphere they inspired and lived in best. The design strategy was to create evocative and unexpected graphic identities for each blend while still linking them back to the Starbucks brand.

The team culled imagery from all over the world to fashion colorful, dynamic collages that capture the essence and personality of a coffee's country of origin or a blend's signature theme. Distinctive colors and icons indigenous to the envisioned "place" a certain coffee bean has journeyed from—for instance, the local flora, fauna, architecture, and art dance in mural compositions around the package's glossy surface. The images are layered to tell a story about the specific blend's unique flavor. Choices range from Romesso, hinting at the coffee's distinctive Italian flair, to Kahawa, an African blend, to names such as Promenade and Studio that cater, respectively, to the look and feel of an uptown kitchen counter or an artist's paint-splattered work room.

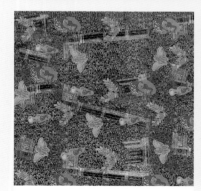

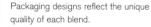
Packaging designs reflect the unique quality of each blend.

"Each design satisfies not just the taste of a specific blend but also the atmosphere in which that blend is likely to be enjoyed. The story it tells completes the experience; it is the bridge between brand and customer."

—Marc Gobé

Each blend owns a unique visual territory made up of imagery evocative of the coffee's country of origin and its distinct personality.

TOUR DE FRANCE

Now more than one hundred years old, the Tour de France has become a mythic event with worldwide visibility, attracting more and more sponsors every year. When the organization contacted Desgrippes Gobé in 1993, the question was how to restore the Tour's image, since it had been cannibalized by the massive influx of sponsor presences. Because each sponsor owns a certain territory of the event—Fiat the finish line, Crédit Lyonnais the podium, Coca-Cola the caravan, and so on—the Tour's identity had been greatly diluted, lacking a powerful, cohesive presence. At the same time, these important sponsors make the tour possible by contributing the finances needed to organize the event and demand visibility as a return on their investment.

Desgrippes Gobé's objective was to give the Tour de France a singular vision, one that was comprehensive and that could be extended into a multi-tiered communications platform under a unified logo. The design concept included an updated visual identity, poster imagery, and architecture designed for the different stages of the racecourse.

Inflatable Personality

Desgrippes Gobé proposed the creation of architectural elements that would appear at important points along each segment of the course, visually joining together different sponsor logos and thus reinforcing the bond between them. The general concept was to produce inflatable structures that could be easily transported and deployed every morning upon the Tour's arrival in a new city. The structures were designed to be inflated directly from the trucks that carried them. Apart from being a highly creative solution, then, the design was also a real technical challenge, as Desgrippes Gobé had to search out a partner who could produce the structural elements while meeting the demanding requirements of their construction.

"The concept of an air-filled structure is truly innovative and gives the event an extraordinarily distinctive scope," says Alain Doré, creative director of Desgrippes Gobé Paris. "The structures float above the heads of the crowd, expanding

Inflatable architectural elements positioned along the Tour route provide a visual link between sponsor logos and a recognizable identity item for the Tour de France in general.

Here Coca-Cola makes its presence known on an inflatable arch over the tour route.

The structures are easily transported and deployed upon arrival in a new city along the Tour by inflating them directly from the trucks that carry them. A launch ramp provides a dramatic backdrop and red-carpet treatment for competitors.

"The concept of an air-filled structure is truly innovative and gives the event an extraordinarily distinctive scope. The structures float above the heads of the crowd, expanding the world of the race into the atmosphere and providing incomparable visibility for the brandmarks they carry."

—Alain Doré, Creative Director, Desgrippes Gobé Paris

the world of the race into the atmosphere and providing incomparable visibility for the brandmarks they carry." Each architectural component acts as both a symbol of the Tour de France and as a visible emblem of the Tour's sponsors. From starting ramp to finish line to awards podium, the pieces share common characteristics, such as the tubular curved overhang, connecting different logos visually in an aesthetically balanced way.

The high visibility of the structures made them a major selling point for the sponsors, as they prominantly display the logos by adapting them to fit their different design elements. Because the Tour de France is such a major television event, the logos had to appear in certain sizes to read clearly for TV viewers. This meant providing them with a space where they were neither too small nor too large to fit inside the camera frame. In the new identity program, the logos are fully integrated into the architectural elements themselves so that they are always visible, providing ideal product-placement opportunities.

The Tour de France is also an emotional event that features televised motivational close-ups of cyclists and audience members, so it was important that sponsor logos blend into the TV format and not interfere in the moment. Desgrippes Gobé organized each sign so that it would appear in just the right spot for maximum visibility, balance, and effect. Ultimately, the new identity program accomplished two goals: to create a real emotional platform for the event through the force of its image and to give its elements greater visibility in an urban environment.

The Tour de France logo is prominently displayed over the finish line on silver and blue inflatable balloons, tying the design back into the overall visual system. Fiat, as sponsor of the finish line, gets a spot for its logo, along with Coca-Cola.

A detail of one of the inflatable structures illustrates the complexity of the
designs.

The awards podium is also assembled quickly at the end of each stage,
creating an impressive mini stadium bearing the Tour de France colors
and logo identity.

TRAVELOCITY

If you were to compare Travelocity's old logo side by side with the new, it would be difficult to say more about the change the brand has undergone. The old logo was limiting in that it showed only airplane travel. Travelocity also offers rail, cruise, even hot air balloon trips, as well as books. The logo needed to capture the excitement of the travel experience. The black, edgy lines of the company's first logo, depicting the New York City skyline, seem a world away from the vibrant blues and orange of the logo Desgrippes Gobé created for the online travel-planning firm. There is an airy quality in tune with the business at hand (flight to faraway destinations) that exists in the gestural star motif, the crisp white lettering on a clear blue sky. These elements convey Travelocity's new sense of youth and buoyancy; they say to the world, "This company is going places."

Optimizing a Brand from the Inside Out

Jeff Glueck, Travelocity's CMO, describes the transformation this way. When he first joined the company, he says, "We were in a business that was technologically driven, with no commitment to make people's experiences valuable. Our business was technical, transactional, and disconnected, and our guests treated us like a commodity. We did not have any loyalty in return." In other words, Travelocity had lost its pole position among competitors, and its new services were not even known, much less considered.

"The company was up for a serious makeover," says Marc Gobé, who oversaw the program. "The brand needed to connect emotionally with people again." Desgrippes Gobé came onboard to create not only a new visual identity but also an entirely new brand positioning and architecture—one built from the ground up and present in each and every expression of the brand, from its corporate identity to its online signature system to its service to customers.

Glueck, along with president and CEO Michelle Peluso, set out to infuse Travelocity with their own passions for entrepreneurship and travel, believing that the best way to reinvigorate the business was to inspire its employees to feel the same way they did about its unique contributions. By reenergizing the people behind the organization and fueling them with the excitement of entrepreneurship, they could bring optimism back into online travel booking and make a significant market difference. "Our gut was telling us that we needed to be about 'optimism,'" remembers Glueck, "and all we were hearing was same old, same old." The change needed to be "inside out," he likes to say.

This kind of contagious energy that motivates a successful brand take-off is precisely what Desgrippes Gobé is so good at generating. The first step was to find out exactly what emotions motivated Travelocity employees, management, and stakeholders, what emotions inspired their own dreams. By extension, those same dreams would motivate and inspire their guests. Through Brand Focus, a visually based brand-building process, Desgrippes Gobé carried out one-on-one interviews with management and conducted group sessions with global stakeholders to craft an appropriate emotional platform and narrative for the brand's future. With the team united around a brand promise in an emotionally engaged way, the sky truly was the limit.

Wishing on a Star

Brand Focus helped the Travelocity group recognize the changes that needed to be made and the steps it needed to take to express its passion to the world. The sessions led to an articulation of an inspiring emotional brand narrative, which in turn led to the new logo design. "From an emotional perspective, we wanted the new logo to be more about possibilities," says Gobé. "We wanted it to suggest that it can help you transcend your normal life. So we needed to express a sense of magic, discovery, imagination, freedom and limitless boundaries."

The designers began by considering symbolism that would suggest dreams, and the notion of wishing on a star emerged as a strong favorite. The solution was a trio of stars drawn loosely in a gestural way and complimented by a simple sans-serif signature to make the logo more personal and approachable. "For thousands of years, travelers have used the stars for navigation," explains Gobé. "The friendly, hand-drawn

The restyled Travelocity logo conveys the "wishing on a star" concept with optimistic blue and orange colors, a refreshing break from the company's original logo, which was confined to darker colors and an urban-skyline theme.

"Traveling is indeed something bigger than the destination: it reveals who we are and our need to renew our love for life and our appetite to connect with others through the stimulation of different cultures."

—Marc Gobé

Original logo

stars and sophisticated colors distinguish Travelocity from its competitors. The stars reflect Travelocity's ability to guide customers to the best trips possible."

In terms of color, the team chose blue to signify open skies and orange to communicate energy. "Orange is a very optimistic color," Gobé notes. "It's a transformative color, associated with the sun, so it is warm and it glows."

The logo design also owes part of its origin to Antoine de St. Exupéry's classic book *The Little Prince*, which provides the perfect metaphor for a young, thoughtful firm such as Travelocity. "Traveling is indeed something bigger than the destination," says Gobé. "It reveals who we are and our need to renew our love for life and our appetite to connect with others through the stimulation of different cultures." Indeed, why else do we travel?

From Mark to Market

It is one thing to create an emotional identity, and another to deliver on the promise of that identity. Even before the new logo was created, Travelocity had already made major strides in its commitment to travelers, but these were yet to be appropriately communicated to guests. Services such as booking travelers at another hotel free of charge if they are dissatisfied with a hotel Travelocity has chosen for them, as well as Travelocity's unique virtual system for making electronic hotel reservations while its competitors fax them, are only two of the services that needed to be talked about.

A major edge Travelocity has over other online travel-planning firms is that rather than list or describe a possible destination, the company sends representatives there to audit the location for specific criteria. Its site, then, doesn't just provide canned sales information, it offers descriptions that actually analyze destinations. This, combined with the "Travelocity Guarantee"—a commitment to be with customers whenever and wherever unexpected problems arise through a team of 2,000 professionals on call 24/7—gives guests an extra sense of trust in the company.

The new logo literally changed the face of the business. In the first three months after the campaign was launched, traffic to the Travelocity website jumped thirty-seven percent from the previous year. The entire site has adopted the same spirit as the logo: It is now about discovery.

Travelocity's website displays bright offerings against its signature rich-blue color and gestural star motif.

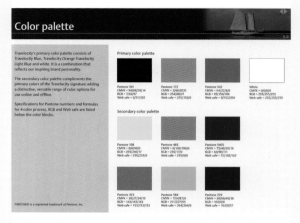

Color palettes are just one of the elements that the Travelocity's corporate-identity guidelines highlight.

The Travelocity business card is simple in execution, but a clear expression of the brand's personality.

The best trips start here.

www.travelocity.com

Sam Gilliland
President and CEO

15100 Trinity Blvd, Fort Worth, TX 76155
Fax: 817 785 8003 Tel: 817 785 8000
sam.gilliland@travelocity.com
www.travelocity.com

FLIGHTS   HOTEL   VACATIONS   CARS   RAIL   VACATIONS   LAST MINUTE DEALS   HELP

Dear Thomas,
Are you ready for your trip to Albuquerque, NM? I've put together
...trip. View your itinerary or
...need to know, things to
...events, you name it.

travelocity
the best trips start here

travelocity   travelocity

Sam Gilliland
PRESIDENT & CEO

T 817 785.8000
F 817 785.8003
sam.gilliland@travelocity.com

15100 Trinity Blvd
Fort Worth, TX 76155
www.travelocity.com

15100

travelocity
the best trips start here

Proposals for logo, signage, website, and business cards using a bright orange background
to help the Travelocity blue pop were ultimately rejected for the blue and orange star logo, as
was an identity system incorporating a hot-air balloon motif.

VP BANK

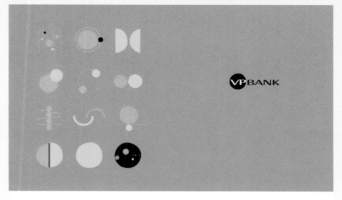

For a small private bank in Lichtenstein, VP Bank has taken gigantic steps to rebrand itself. Because of a need for more transparency in the country's banking operations, stricter regulations had been imposed and banking in Lichtenstein had become less attractive to Europeans. In order to counter the trend and appeal again to new customers, VP Bank wanted to stand out as a viable option by conveying a coherent and, above all, human message. The new brand message would give people a reason to choose VP Bank over its competitors.

Not only did Desgrippes Gobé create this message for the bank, along with the unique graphic styling and visual identity to communicate it, but it also fashioned a total brand consciousness for VP Bank, a personality that would be recognizable the minute a customer stepped into the branch.

Welcome to the World of Unusual and Elegant Banking

Desgrippes Gobé studied VP Bank closely to gain a full and intimate understanding of its emotional presence. This deep examination fed into the creation of a graphic identity and brand icon aligned with the bank's values and vision for the future. Inspired by the haute-couture universe Desgrippes Gobé knows so well the new brand identity blends a contemporary high-art grace with a definitively humanistic and handcrafted look to express the brand as upscale but also endlessly warm and approachable, unusual and elegant. The team simplified the name to its initials (from the Verwaltungs und Privat-Bank) to give it the candor of a nickname, and designed every element of the new positioning, from logo to visual identity to publications to branch architecture.

"Before, potential customers would have probably wondered, 'If I had money to put in the bank, I don't know why I would choose VP Bank,'" points out François Caratgé. "Now, the reasons are evident: VP Bank's singular identity has real brand value and a unique positioning."

A big part of this positioning is its atypical qualities. Normally, banking institutions draw heavily from corporate, authoritarian elements that can be dry and cold in nature.

In order to identify VP Bank as anything but a stuffy financial institution, the vocabulary developed for the new identity contains no straight lines or angles, and no mechanical or cold elements. As though drawn by hand, the shapes are decidedly imperfect, providing idiosyncratic visual symbols and colors that express partnership, proximity, relationships, trust, and the notion of being tailor-made. Even the circle—the nucleus for all other designs—is charmingly asymmetrical.

VP Bank goes an entirely different route in its visual identity, where forms are not precise but distinct, abstract, human-like shapes floating in space. With fine, dynamic yet hand-drawn lines, where a circle isn't perfectly round and forms appear slightly off-center, the new VP Bank imagery differentiates itself by aligning more with the high-art world of painting and fashion than it does with a stuffy, imposing banking institution.

Creating a Disturbance

Desgrippes Gobé innovated a graphic vocabulary that would express the bank's ability to form friendly partnerships with clients and offer guidance without relying heavily on statistics and performance figures, as other banks commonly do. The vocabulary developed for the new identity does not contain any angles or straight lines, no mechanical or cold industrial elements. Instead, the shapes are decidedly imperfect, as though they have been drawn by hand. From these idiosyncratic visual symbols, VP

Crafted in stylish yet human colors, a sales brochure features a simple circle shape in orange and yellow symbolic of the sun and the concept of synergy.

Bank's new vocabulary emerges, emphasizing themes such as partnership, proximity, relationships, tailor-made, and trust. The circle acts as the nucleus for all of the other designs.

Paired with the imagery are black-and-white photographs candidly capturing everyday business transactions to show the natural skills VP Bank possesses. Not only are there real, live people behind this bank, but they are also people with smiles on their faces: they are young and professional-looking, enthusiastic and dependable. The photographs convey a more specific, authentic, and transparent aspect of the design and create a surprising and unconventional twist on ordinary bank visuals. "Usually the banking universe uses the strong black-and-white contrast in its more abstract elements, to convey its corporate symbol, not its photographs of people," explains Elie Hasbani, creative director at Desgrippes Gobé Paris. "But VP Bank turns this tired protocol on its head, introducing color where it isn't normally expected and black and white where it isn't expected either."

The black-and-white imagery also serves to highlight the unusual color combinations that make the VP Bank visual identity stand out. The choice of the color system was of utmost importance to Desgrippes Gobé. Selecting a natural skin tone as the base—a color that is warm as well as chic, reminiscent of high fashion—the team bounced off brighter lime green, tangerine orange, and crimson. The colors are elementary and sophisticated at the same time, hearkening back to the hand-tailored appeal of fine clothing and accessories as well as high-quality art.

This was a completely unprecedented move in the world of private banking, bringing VP Bank to the forefront of its category even though it was small in size. "Our objective was to create a disturbance in the banking universe with a more creative approach and the strong affirmation that 'small is indeed beautiful,'" says Hasbani.

"In a context of rapidly changing rules and regulations, the only alternative was to come up with one or more significant reasons why banking customers should prefer VP Bank. In other words, we had to create a brand."

—François Caratgé,
General Manager, Desgrippes Gobé Paris

Left: Designs for the stylish VP Bank interior incorporate warm skin tones and brighter accents, as well as distinctively contemporary architectural elements. The themes of high art and design are noticeably suggested in wall paintings hung behind the desks and other fashionable elements such as couches and standing lamps.

Right: Business-card designs feature the reconceived logo evocative of the bank's credibility and strength while also introducing warmer, more natural letterforms and coloring.

WEIGHT WATCHERS

In the age of emotional branding, a logo becomes more than a clever doodle: it is the articulation of how a company feels about what it does. As a carrier of emotion, a logo has the challenge of conveying those feelings to the world and upholding them in countless situations and communications. Weight Watchers as a company is itself about emotions—in particular, a person's feelings around being overweight and the frustration entailed in trying to overcome obstacles to a more fit and healthy body. When Desgrippes Gobé took on the redesign of the organization's logo, the goal was to create an image that honestly addresses the feelings of Weight Watchers customers and instills in them a message of hope.

Logo Power

"An emotional brand like Weight Watchers needed a powerful logo, an iconic representation of the company's commitment to its customers," asserts Marc Gobé. "As a global organization, it was important that the new logo not be just a marker or a recognizable signature but also the expression of the group's passionate leadership." The search was for a type of visual symbol and typographic expression that breathed a sense of optimism and pride and could be appropriated by staff and customers alike. The creation of the new logo would have to be an inside-out job, motivated by top management to show the true essence of who and what they were about.

"Our name is a message, a meaning, and a promise," emphasizes Weight Watchers president, Linda Huett. "Our logo needed to reflect the profound emotions attached to the brand by our guests and the life-changing experiences people have with us." Weight Watchers is not a beauty company; it does not sell firming creams, nor is it a toothpaste company promising a whiter smile. The company deals with the most profound of emotions, the depth of people's psyches and what is really "you." Most Weight Watchers customers walking through the door have already recognized, either consciously or unconsciously, that they have at least fifty pounds to lose and a history of failure with other dieting approaches. Weight Watchers offers them a new chance to solve the problem, to change their lives.

From Vision to Visual Message

Desgrippes Gobé conducted Brand Focus with the group's management to help them unearth visuals that would inspire the new logo. One visual in particular captured their attention. It was a picture of a hand pulling back a white curtain in an unlit room. Showing through the window was a green lawn on what appeared to be a sunny day. This visual attracted all members of the Weight Watchers team because of its powerful metaphor of darkness versus light and the underlying message that there is always a possible solution. The essence of the visual was then translated into the logo.

The logo design depicts a wave of color, transitioning from dark blue to light green to yellow in a circular motion. The cyclical movement of the design speaks to the never-ending cycles in people's lives. "The wave represents the essence of Weight Watchers—the sense of empowerment, energy, and transformation," explains Peter Levine. "Visually, the arcs of the wave, going from dark to light in color, illustrate the Weight Watchers experience and underscore the brand's attributes. The blue arc conveys the strength and support provided by the Weight Watchers community, the green signifies healthy living, and the yellow represents the idea of a dawn of a new day and the sense of rejuvenation. At Weight Watchers, every day is about renewal and a fresh start to a healthy way of living."

For the message to be understood, it needed to be expressed in each and every aspect of the Weight Watchers communication, from image to color choice to the typography of the wordmark. "The symbol conveys a feeling of hope, with the colors moving from darkness to light," Huett points out. "It says also that you are never finished. The typography is genderless and friendly in a blue color that is positive in every market."

A strong understanding of the emotional identity a company projects to the outside world is crucial if it is to connect in a more personal way. "To be successful it has to care more than any business, it has to accept its mission with the greatest integrity and love," adds Gobé. "The Weight Watchers brand is a trust brand in its purest form, a brand based on the values

WeightWatchers®

The Weight Watchers logo incorporates a dynamic wave design in colors transitioning from dark blue to light green to yellow in an optimistic, circular motion, which speaks to the continuous cycle of life in many different languages.

"Our name is a message, a meaning, and a promise. Our logo needed to reflect the profound emotions attached to the brand by our guests and the life-changing experiences people have with us. The symbol conveys a feeling of hope."

—Linda Huett, President, Weight Watchers

of safety, ethics, and stewardship." The new identity has helped the brand overcome one of its biggest challenges as a business: its customers' struggle with denial. Weight Watchers encourages guests to work toward self-realization and guides them in defeating denial, but this can only happen in a trusted environment. The logo helps to reinforce the message that Weight Watchers is there to support and care for its customers.

Communicating Hope

The nature of the Weight Watchers organization is to leverage the power of connection through group meetings, as well as to provide a wide array of products and services tailored to the individual. The refreshed logo and wordmark were adapted to all communications of the brand—from packaging labels to the Weight Watchers magazine masthead to the brand's on-shelf presence in retail environments and even on the Web. Desgrippes Gobé crafted detailed guidelines for future communications, providing an extended color palette and alternative typographic adjustments that could be made for different uses. Through and through, the emotional identity conveyed by the logo offers relief and reinforces the company's commitment to its profoundly caring approach.

Label designs expand upon the wave motif and blue and green colors.

Signage for a Weight Watchers center mirrors the logo design.

Weight Watchers packaging designs convey the variety of food items available while tying back into the visual identity.

Colors

The consistent use of color in the Weight Watchers logo is an important element in establishing a memorable corporate identity. Therefore, Weight Watchers blue, Weight Watchers green, and Weight Watchers yellow have been selected as the corporate logo colors. These colors can't be altered under any circumstances.

The color chips below represent the Weight Watchers logo colors. For use in print, use the Pantone® colors listed below the color chips or their equivalents using the 4-color process colors. For use on the Weight Watchers web site, the appropriate color codes are also given.

	Weight Watchers BLUE	Weight Watchers GREEN	Weight Watchers YELLOW
PANTONE COATED	PMS 287 C	PMS 368 C	PMS 116 C
PANTONE UNCOATED	PMS 287 U	PMS 368 U	PMS 109 U
PROCESS COLORS	C100 M70 Y0 K10	C65 M0 Y86 K0	C0 M15 Y100 K0
WEB COLORS	R0 G61 B153	R102 G204 B51	R255 G204 B0

*Pantone® is a registered trademark of Pantone, Inc.

WeightWatchers®

Weight Watchers International, Inc.
175 Crossways Park West
Woodbury, NY 11797-2055
Phone: 516-390-1400 • Fax: 516-390-1445
Email: jsmith@weight-watchers.com

JOSEPH M. SMITH
Vice President, Marketing

A page from the Weight Watchers corporate identity guidelines delineates the logo color palette as illustrated in the corporate stationery and business cards.

THE WORLD GOLF HALL OF FAME

Often brand design takes on more than a single product to confront a concept and reinvent an entire category. This is what Marc Gobé and his New York team achieved for the World Golf Hall of Fame in St. Augustine, Florida. Here was a place that housed not just a sporting event but an experience of golf's rich heritage and history. It was this experience—not a golf club or ball—that needed to take part in the brand-design process. Desgrippes Gobé's challenge was to think beyond the parameters of the industry and emphasize that golf was much more than a sport, but a full-sensory entertainment experience. The team designed the visual identity and insignia for the Hall of Fame as well as signage, stationery, and logo for the World Golf Village resort that has been built around it.

All in One: From Sport to Experience

The game of golf is something avid players and professionals don't have to quantify: it is simply an experience that keeps them returning to the golf course week after week, year after year. Maybe it has to do with the outdoor nature of the sport, the rolling greens and crisp curves of the course, the rush of driving a ball hundreds of yards through the air. Whatever it is that stirs such passion for the game has inspired the creation of a world destination where enthusiasts can literally live the life of golf as well as share in honoring its past.

"In creating the logo for the World Golf Hall of Fame, it was important both to celebrate the tradition of golf and its inspiring history and at the same time not to forget that the game is also for the future," says Marc Gobé, who was the lead designer on the project and is himself a golf enthusiast. Gobé wanted to capture the humanistic side of the game, the passion for competition out-of-doors, an undying love of the challenge. "Golf is accessible and a fun sport, even for a younger generation," Gobé insists. "The logo incorporates not only a traditional feel, but also gestures that are spirited and dynamic." When pinned or monogrammed onto a jacket, the logo becomes a symbol of membership in this world-class community.

Gobé selected the coat of arms as the insignia for the World Golf Hall of Fame, where close to one hundred of the sport's greats are commemorated. The brandmark, with its navy, forest-green, and burgundy coloring, evokes golf's early origins in medieval Scotland, where the game enjoyed the regal atmosphere of royal tournaments, much as it still does today. In fact, the first exhibit in the Hall of Fame museum, designed by the eminent architect Ralph Appelbaum, is heralded by the echoing sounds of bagpipes ushering visitors toward the display. The coat of arms visual is paired with a modern typeface in a sunny gold color and crowned by a gestural sketch of the Hall of Fame and catchy hand-drawn stars.

The logo Desgrippes Gobé designed for the World Golf Village also has this hand-drawn quality, the look of penmanship whipped out in a moment of joy and inspiration. The lines river into the shape of a putting green with again the Hall of Fame rotunda set off in the distance. The colors are kept simple and clean: the green of the course, the red of rank and distinction, and the black for impact. The logo simultaneously conveys a sense of playfulness and old-fashioned assurance; it knows its audience and speaks directly to them. Extending the royal tournament theme, white flags proudly flying the World Golf Village's logo are placed as signage and location markers throughout the resort.

Inspired by a coat of arms, the logo design for the World Golf Hall of Fame evokes the sport's origins in medieval Scotland. The navy blue, forest green, and burgundy communicate the regal atmosphere in which the game has tradition-ally been played, but the modern gold typeface and hand-drawn illustration lend a contemporary freshness.

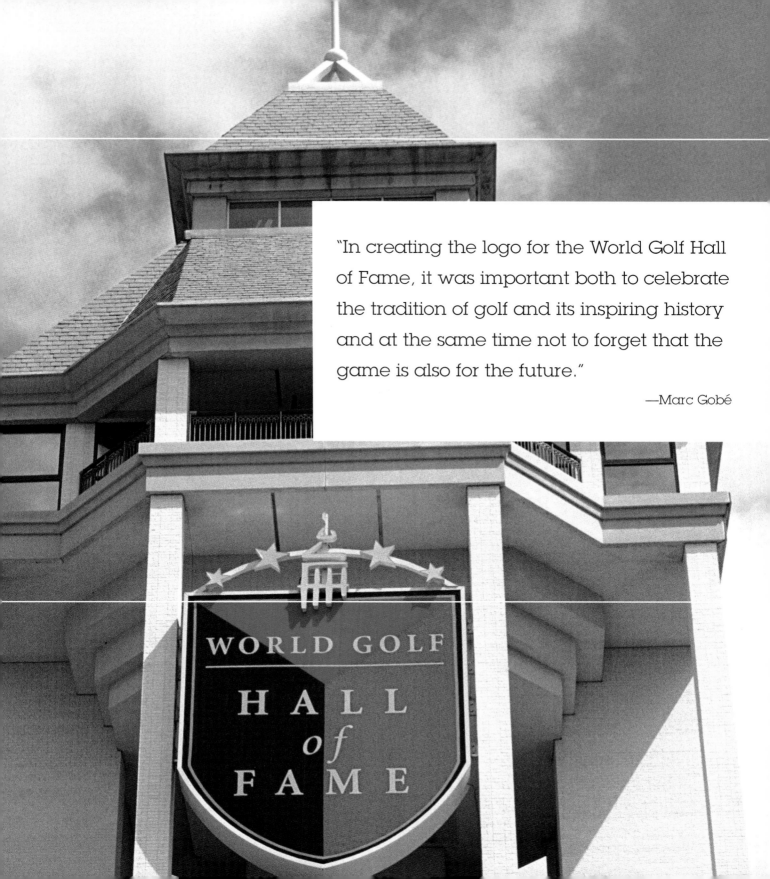

"In creating the logo for the World Golf Hall of Fame, it was important both to celebrate the tradition of golf and its inspiring history and at the same time not to forget that the game is also for the future."

—Marc Gobé

WORLD GOLF
VILLAGE

The World Golf Village logo has a hand-drawn, gestural quality, with fluid lines that shape the putting green and Hall of Fame rotunda in red. In slight contrast, the classic typography upholds the tradition and cultural distinction of the sport.

A logo for the World Golf Village golf course conveys a sense of both play-fulness and old-fashioned assurance with strong, black "strokes" and a simple, hand-drawn design.

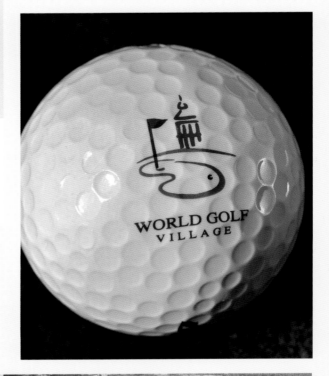

The logos for the World Golf Village and World of Golf Hall of Fame are a versatile design that rests easily on a variety of gift items from hats and shirts to key chains and golf balls.

The World Golf Hall of Fame, with its tall turreted rotunda, sits at the center of the World Golf Village in St. Augustine, Florida.

World Golf Hall of Fame members gather together sporting their jackets, each emblazoned with the Hall of Fame logo.

The turreted rotunda of the World Golf Hall of Fame is modern and at the same time evocative of golf's origins. The coat of arms logo stands out against the white columns of the structure. The circular pool in front (12) is designed in the shape of the globe, with different continents placed throughout, symbolizing the sport's worldwide reach.

Gestural logo drawings for the Word Golf Village highlight in white on black the world-class facilities, international online presence, and distinctive architecture of this prized golf destination.

WORLD MARCH

Fashion and comfort are well-known incompatibles, especially in the shoe department. But for Moonstar, Japan's leading shoe manufacturer, comfort was key, and it took pride in its unique walking-shoe technology called Walking Saver. However, design-wise these shoes failed to register on the fashion radar, and were viewed as unstylish and out of date. The Desgrippes Gobé Tokyo team stepped in to clarify the World March brand identity and give its design presence a little kick.

Designing Lines

Desgrippes Gobé first divided the World March comfort shoe into three categories: Male Style-walking, Female Style-walking, and Sport-walking. The team conducted Brand Focus to define the visual territory of each category and build a cohesive identity for the brand. It also reactivated and highlighted Walking Saver, Moonstar's unique technology for building the perfect walking shoe that every World March product offers. Desgrippes Gobé leveraged the Walking Saver technology to create a powerful synergy between design and comfort in the new shoe, making it incomparable to others on the market.

"We helped Moonstar focus on stylish shoe design rather than solely comfort-oriented design," says Yoko Margaret Iwasaki, creative strategist Desgrippes Gobé Tokyo. "By leveraging not just the technology behind the shoe but also its fashion sense, we created an unbeatable presence for World March in the shoe category."

A Marching Logo

After defining the World March brand identity and visual territory, the team created the World March brand logo, six product brand logos, and the Walking Saver logo. World March now has a brandmark that boasts stylish orange and earth-gray coloring and striking white script, which Desgrippes Gobé calls the "dynamic string." The orange meets the gray to form a horizon from which emerges the white scribble of "WM," giving it the illusion that the brand name is marching toward you. Simple and clean, the logo feels light and full of motion, while the contrasting background and modern World March typeface anchors it in the present moment. Both the horizon line and dynamic string are reiterated on shoeboxes, shopping bags, and in-store displays, and in all marketing materials—posters, brochures, and even promotional doormats.

Imagery for sales brochures conveys the comfort of wearing World March shoes and their context in the natural environment.

World March's online presence keeps colors modern and simple, in earth tones, while utilizing the "dynamic string" letterforms of the logo.

Signage in the World March store emphasizes the horizon line and "dynamic string" script Desgrippes Gobé invented for the brand.

Shopping bags and shoe boxes pair contemporary, earthbound colors to create a simplified horizon line, cutting the surface in half. The white scribble moniker appears to "walk" across the picture plain, and crisp lettering identifies the brand.

Imagery for binders and other business materials carries the warm colors and horizon-line design of the brand's visual identity.

In-shop stools double as display shelves.

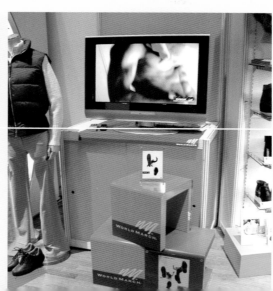

An in-store video screen blends into the modern feel of the retail environment.

XL LOUNGE

Desgrippes Gobé's design for the XL Lounge in New York City could qualify as a designer's dream job. The commission was to take a raw industrial space and transform it into a cutting-edge watering hole. Given free rein over the design concept, the Desgrippes Gobé team created a premium, luxurious lounge that transcended the traditional downtown club scene, the kind of place that enticed customers in for an after-work drink and encouraged them to stay until the morning hours.

Designing from the Imagination

The team dreamed up an imaginative space that consistently provides a fashionable, upscale aura. Designing each room with the feelings of patrons in mind, they divided the space into emotional zones that morph and adapt to fit particular moods and ultimately lift customers' spirits. A sophisticated computer-controlled lighting system was installed so that the lighting subtly changes according to the music or vibe the bar wants to project.

State-of-the-art materials fabricate an experience that is chic in every sense, including the latest in video technology decorating the walls as well as a cool and crisp combination of metal and glass construction, underscoring the ultra-modern nature of the bar. Paired with the high-tech feel, however, are distinctly natural elements, such as a fish-filled aquarium wall in the bathrooms and a VIP room crowned by a trompe l'oeil sky ceiling, complete with wistful white clouds on a perfectly pale-blue background. There are multiple hang-out areas to choose from, each tailored to different bar-setting desires, from minimalist stools studding a futuristic bar island to plush benches and more intimate, closed-off corners offering comfortable leather seating, wood-paneled walls, and private TV screens.

"We wanted to create a concept that is utterly unconventional in a category that is overcrowded with too much of the same old same old," says Sam O'Donahue, lead designer on the project. "Most of all, we wanted to create a lounge atmosphere that exudes sophistication and harnesses state-of-the-art technology to create a powerful emotional experience."

Not only did the team conceive of and implement the design from raw garage space to finished lounge, it also commandeered the bar's strategic positioning, which included its unique architecture as well as supporting brand communication materials.

The futuristic bar island lined with minimalist square stools glows with recessed lighting in deep blue and aqua.

Upstairs, a trompe l'oeil sky ceiling imparts a soothing vibe as well as a stylish setting in which to sip cocktails.

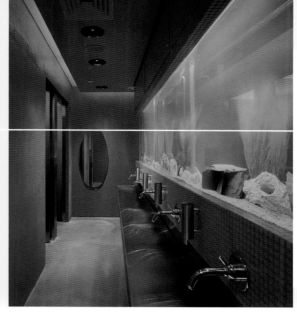

"We wanted to create a concept that is utterly unconventional in a category that is overcrowded with too much of the same old same old. Most of all, we wanted to create a lounge atmosphere that exudes sophistication and harnesses state-of-the-art technology to create a powerful emotional experience."

—Sam O'Donahue, Design Director, Desgrippes Gobé New York

Conclusion

Getting to Know You

Emotional brand design is everywhere—not just in the tangible realm of products and services but also in the invisible, intangible realm of auras and personalities. It is in those attributes that don't always cooperate with words but that can be felt through a certain color, taste, touch, or scent. When you realize what emotional brand design is, by seeing it implemented in Desgrippes Gobé projects around the world, you realize just how pervasive it is not just throughout space but throughout time. At the core of emotional branding is a concept that has always existed: the concept of introducing yourself to others, getting to know others as they get to know you. It's the notion of connection, that we are all somehow connected, whether we live in New York or in Hong Kong, in Brussels or Seoul, whether we prefer one activity to another or like one thing and dislike something else. Chances are, there is at least one other person out in the world who understands us better than we understand ourselves, by being a good friend, by listening to us, by watching us grow. Branding is like this: it is finding the personality within a product or service and introducing it to others, helping the brand get to know others as they get to know the brand. This concept is universal, and it is eternal.

On the other hand, emotional brand design has really been around for only about thirty-five years. It is startlingly fresh, in fact, a seed of something much larger that is just now breaking the surface and beginning to bloom. Design agencies and advertising firms are catching on to this trend in brand design, because, simply, they have to. It's what branding is all about—getting to know people, letting them get to know you. When I look at the pantheon of designs Desgrippes Gobé has completed, I am amazed by the cutting-edge, sometimes even radical, thinking behind them. And yet, at the same time, how fundamental the initial intent is: to bring humanity closer together.

We are already seeing the effects of emotional brand design in our lives, in the stores we like to shop in, the clothes we wear, the music we listen to, the places where we spend most of our time, whether at the office, in the home, or outside in the natural environment. I don't think it is too optimistic to say that things are coming together, getting a little more harmonious each day. We are seeing people of all backgrounds, whether racial, social, or sexual, interconnecting, forming communities, raising families. Although this of course is not the whole picture (as war and violence and separation continue to play a part in our daily lives), I think it is safe to say that it is an expanding one, a "whole picture" that was not there even twenty years ago and that is steadily growing larger in aperture to contain more and more people.

I walk into spaces now that are not only beautifully designed in terms of furniture, lighting, or wall color, but also in their scents, the music that whispers through their sound systems. I walk through parks that post better-designed garbage bins, and more of them, as well as those that provide recycling options. I ride in cars engineered to use less fuel, visit houses with geothermal temperature systems, operate machines designed to use less electricity. I am learning that the key to efficiency is design, that the reverse is not the only truth. We need design. We need something that continually keeps our minds in check, pushes us to perfect what we use and how we use it. Without it, what waste—of time, of energy, of mind space, all things we can put to a better purpose: getting to know others and letting them get to know us.

About the Writer

Anne Hellman is a writer living in Brooklyn, New York. She is the editor of *Brandjam* by Marc Gobé (Allworth Press) and of *In the Pink: Dorothy Draper, America's Most Fabulous Decorator* by Carleton Varney and *Class Act: William Haines, Legendary Hollywood Decorator* by Peter Schifando (both Pointed Leaf Press).

Desgrippes Gobé Employees

We are grateful as well to all those who have worked with Desgrippes Gobé along the way and whose names we may have unintentionally forgotten to mention.

ACCART François
ACHADE Muriel
ACHARD Sylviane
ADIAN Michael A.
AGEORGES Christele
AH KIM Jung
AIRAUD Rodolphe
AIRES Maria Luisa
AIRES Ricardo
AIZAWA Ryoko
AKASAKA Chieko
ALLEN Sarah
ALVAREZ Sara
AMIOT Armelle
ANCELY Dominique
ANDRAULT Lise
ANGLARES Michele
AOKI Maiko
APHEZBERRO Martine
APOSTOLOWSKA Magda
ARAGAKI Phyllis
ASCANI Michael
ASHEN David
ASSAYAG Yael
ATIENZA Marie-France
AUBIN Eric
AUBOSSU Marc
AUCLAIR Marielle
AUDINEAU Mariele
AUFAURE Murielle
AUFFREDO Jean-Pierre
AUGUSTYNIAK Mathieu
AZELSON-CHIDSEY Eliza
AZZOLINI Remy
BABANSKYJ Larissa
BAEGENS Sylvaine

BAGUES Josianne
BAILLET Veronique
BAILLOU Alain
BALARD Jean-Claude
BALDWIN Elizabeth
BALIGAND Frederique
BALLENTINE-SCOTT Molly
BANCELIN Magalie
BANDOLO Claire
BANKS Lisa
BAPTISTE Roseline
BARANGER Cyrille
BARBARESI Josianne
BARBOZA Raoul
BARCAT Anne
BARDAT Clarisse
BARIL Dominique
BARILLEY Marie-Aude
BARNES Harriet
BARON Florence
BARON Sylvie
BAROUKH Joselyne
BARREAU Cecile
BATAILLE Marie
BAUDRY Catherine
BAUDUIN Henri
BAUMAN Arnaud
BAUTISTA Ana
BAYER Alain
BAZ Ayed
BEAUCHANT Patrice
BEAULAND Luc
BEBERMAN Erica
BECK Melinda
BEDDAD Carine
BEDOT Regine
BEDOUET Charlotte

BEGUINOT Nathalie
BEHOT Veronique
BELLAMY Chantal
BELLE Dominique
BELLONI Marion
BELORGEY Lydia
BEN TEMELLIST Sadok
BEN YAAGOUB Abderrahman
BENADREAU Florence
BENAISSA Ali
BENAISSA Myriam
BENCHERIF Sophie
BENDER Sara
BENN Alex
BERARD Jerôme
BERARD Jerome E.
BERAS Erasma
BERCE Sonia
BERCOVICI Sandrine
BERESUK Georges
BERKW Carolyn
BERLIN Pascale
BERNARD Françoise
BERNARD Valene
BERSON Susan
BERTHE Muriel
BERTIN Fabrice
BERTOLA Dominique
BESCHER Marie-Beatrice
BESSONET Sarah
BETHEA Ann
BEYER Jr. Emil J.
BEYNET Françoise
BEZ Abderrazak
BIGUET Nathalie
BILLOT Estelle

BILSKI Janna
BINARD Eve
BINISTI Remi
BISPO Auguste
BISSELL Janice
BLAIS Dominique
BLAKE Nathan
BLANC Pricille
BLANC Valerie
BLANCHERE Laure
BLANCHOT Priscilla
BLAT Anne
BLAT Frederic
BLATTNER Wendy
BLAVEC Ingrid
BLOCH Edouard
BLOQUERE Catherine
BLUMENSTEIN Lynn
BOCHE Pascal
BOHDZIUL Kazi
BOILEVIN Christine
BOISSEAU Violette
BOLLMAN Steven
BOMMELAER Delphine
BONNAUD Marie-Frederique
BONNET Catherine
BONNET Marie-Laure
BORGES Viviane
BOSCHETTI Marianne
BOTON Albert
BOTON Florence
BOU Rafael
BOUCHEK Alexandra
BOUCHER Catherine
BOUCHERE Valerie

BOUCHEREAU Colette
BOUCHEZ Françoise
BOUCHOIR Helene
BOUDERHEM Aïcha
BOUDY Eric
BOUEXIERE Laurent
BOUGOUFFA Linda
BOUJU Isabelle
BOULANGER Carole
BOULE Guy
BOULET Fabrice
BOULET Patrice
BOULEY Patrick
BOULOT Caroline
BOURACHOT Laurent
BOURET Muriel
BOURGEOIS Dominique
BOUTILLIER Philippe
BOUVARD Alison
BOUYJOU Christian
BOWLER Kristen
BOYER Vincent
BRAHIMI Sabba
BRAMHANDKAR Dipti
BRANDDENBURG Claudia
BRAUNSCHWEIL Stephanie
BRELIVET Maud
BRENAC Aurelie
BRENNEUR Fabienne
BRIAND Gabriel
BRIARD Marie-Line
BRIEND Geraldine
BRIGGS Craig

BROCHE Sophie
BROESCKE Pascale
BROUANT Isabelle
BROUZES Valerie
BRUANT Lorene
BRUCHON Sylvian
BRUNET Alain
BRUNET Elisabeth
BRUNO Jose
BRUYERE Patrick
BRYCH Marianne
BUDERE Jackie
BUNGARD Brigitta
BURLOT Valerie
BURNS Jennifer
BURRIS James
CABEDO Julian
CABOS Laurence
CABROL Cecile
CACHON Claire
CADENE Christine
CADIOT Christophe
CAHEN Anne
CAIE David
CALLY Corinne
CANESSE Dominique
CANONGE Mario
CANTEL Jean
CANZANI Bruno
CAPLAN Leah
CAPPELLO Ronald
CARATGE François
CARCOPINO Alain
CARLIER Aurélie
CARLIER Olivier
CARRADE DE LUCA Stephane
CARRERA Jean-Philippe
CARRERAS Nathalie

CARSWELL Courtney
CARTIER Marguerite
CARTY Danielle
CASAS Rubin
CASCONE Bernadette
CASE Gail
CATO Mac
CAUGHLIN Thomas
CAVES Erin
CAZARES Alicia
CHABAUD Caroline
CHAILLET Bertille
CHAISE Marie-Françoise
CHALLER Sylvie
CHALLIER Camille
CHALLIER Catherine
CHALLIER Marion
CHAMOLT Martine
CHAN Aimee
CHAN Edith
CHAN Harriet
CHAOUCHE Farid
CHAPUIS Guillaume
CHARBONNIER Helene
CHARBONNIER Luc
CHARLEUX Agnes
CHARRIER Denis
CHARTIER Anne
CHARZAT Claire
CHAULIEU Olivier
CHAUMELY Catherine
CHAYS Pierre-Yves
CHAZERANS Isabelle
CHELEU Lydia
CHEN Yuk-Kuen

CHESNEAU Manuela
CHEVALIER Françoise
CHEVALLIER Brigitte
CHEVALLIER Denys
CHICOT Isabelle
CHIELI Federico
CHIFFLOT Xavier
CHOI Jessica
CHOW Stella
CHRISTOPHER Stephanie
CHUNG Yoon-Sun
CLAISSE Bernard
CLARK Alisa
CLASS Frederic
CLAUSTRE Dalila
CLAVEL Cécile
CLEARBOUT Renaud
CLEARY Lisa
CLEDAT Marianne
CLEMENT Cathy
CLEMENT Priscille
COIL Kimberly
COINTET Veronique
COLE Celine
COLIN Christiane
COLLADO Juan Paul
COLLET Veronique
COMBES Joëlle
COMET Marie-France
CONSANI Anne
CONSTANTINO Arlindo
CONTENCIN Nicole
CORBEL Christine
CORDERO Rafael
CORDIER Herve

CORDON Alain

CORLETO Adam

CORMIER Fabienne

CORNEBIZE Catherine

CORNILLET Eric

CORREA Michelle

COSENTINO Michele

COSNARD Marc

COSSE Nathalie

COTTO Gabriel

COUSSAUD Chantal

COUTANCIER Arnaud

COUTARD Blandine

COUTE Corinne

COUZI Jean-Etienne

CREPON Carole

CRETON Frederique

CROUAN Pascaline

CURUTCHET Aurelie

CUSSAQUET Regine

CVEK Katy

CYHOLNYK Nicolas

DA CUHNA Sandra

DACUMMOC Laurent

DADON Paty Fabienne

D'ALLEMAGNE Christian

DAMERON Patrick

DAMICO Rachel

DANIAU Marc

DANIELS Leighkaren

DANNA Matthew

DANTCHIK Leslie

DAO Jean-Pierre

DARD Florence

D'ARFEUILLE Olivier

DARS Sylvie

DAVID Yaëlle

DAVIDSON Thomas

DAWIDOWICZ Vanessa

DE ALBERGARIA Eduardo

DE BENGUY Sabine

DE BERU Loïc

DE CHASSEY Sabine

DE CLAUZADE Beatrice

DE CLOSMADEVE Geraldine

DE FILIPPO Marc

DE GUZMAN Rafael

DE JOURGUES Isabelle

DE LA PIEDRA Annie

DE LA SELLE Ines

DE LAMBERTERIE Alexandre

DE LARDEMELLE Delphine

DE LEON Richard

DE LEU Cecile

DE LEU Marine

DE LEU Zoe

DE LEUCLOS Nicole

DE LIGT Francis

DE MOING DE TISSOT Christine

DE MULLENHEIM Clotilde

DE NOAILLES Alban

DE PAUL PIQUET Florence

DE PREISSAC Ludovic

DE ROCQUIGNY Anne

DE ROUYN Guillaume

DE SAN JOSE Sandrine

DEBENARDY Anne

DEBON Marc

DECHATRE Olivier

DECITRE Camille

DECONINCK Nicolas

DECRU Anne-Marie

DEFER Laurence

DEGHAYE BAEY-ENS Christine

DEGOUTTE Claude

DEJOU Stephane

DEKETELAERE Jean-Paul

DEL GRUPTA. Sanbit

DEL TEDESCO Laure

DELAFOSSE Anne-Claire

DELALAING Xavier

DELANGE Daniel

DELASSUS Esperance

DELAUNAY Genevieve

DELECLUSE Jeanne

DELEU Roland

DELEU Zoe

DELMAR Jeanne

DELMONT Claire

DELSART Catherine

DELVAUX Pauline

DEMAY Marie-Christine

DEMEZ Emmanuel

DENNIGAN Christine

DEQUIRMEND Nathalie

DERBIN Laure

DERCHAIN Eric

DERMENGHEN Anne

DERVAUX Daniel

DES CLOSETS Nadege

DESAUES Gerard

DESCURE Sandrine

DESGRIPPES Anne-Sophie

DESGRIPPES Annie

DESGRIPPES Caroline

DESGRIPPES Catherine

DESGRIPPES Christine

DESGRIPPES Joël

DESGRIPPES Lise

DESHAIRES Sandrine

DESJOURS Sophie

DESLANDE Elsa

DESOUCHES Elisabeth

DESPREZ Josianne

DESROSIERS Isabelle

DESSANE Sandrine

DESSENNE Sophie

DESTREMAU Dominique

DESVIGNES Fanny

DEVECHE Colette

DEVEZE Iris

DEVILLELE Laure

DEVINAST Richard

DEVLIN James

DEVLIN Stewart

DEVOUGE-LAMI-ELLE Gabrielle

DEWITT Arielle

DIAS Anna

DIEULE Claudia

DION Philippe

DIPSZYC Raymond

DISDERO Nadine

DIZIER Charles

DJOUGONNANGA Kasende

DOBREMEZ Estelle

DOFFOEL Josette

DOISEAU Isabelle

DOLESE Georges

DOMENGE Marc

DOMITTER Christopher M.

DOPPELT Suzanne

DORE Alain

DORE Marine

DORIN Stanislas

DOUANE Eric

DOUAY Gilles

DOUCHIN May

DOUGE Laurence

DOUILLET Sophie

DOUSSOT Stephane

DOUTRELOUX Fanny

DREANO Florence

DREYFUS Annie

DRILLON François

DROUARD Elodie

DROUDE Christian

DROUET Emilie

DUBOS Emmanuel

DUBREUIL Hortense

DUCASSE Maurice

DUCHESNE Marie-Pierre

DUCOUREAU Quitterie

DUFFY John

DUGAST Magali

DUGUET Anne

DUJARDIN Fabienne

DUJARDIN DE LA COUR Diane

DUMONTIER Karine

DUPIN Claire

DUPRE Amandine

DUPRE Sabrina

DUPUIS Florence

DUPUIS Paul

DUPUIS Philippe

DUPUY Eric

DUPUY Paul

DURAND Veronique

DURAND Yves

DURDABAK Elisa

DUREY Florence

DUROYON Veronique

DURY Selene

DUSAUD Yannick

DUSSAZ Robert

D'USSEL Marie-Blanche

DUTHU Emmanuelle

DUVAL Anne-Laure

DUVAL Brian

DUVAL Nicole

DUVIQUET Danielle

ECAL Joselyn

ECKERD Lindsey

EDEB Jean-Hamid

EDMOND Jean

EDOUARD Josette

EFINGER Tanner

EL MZIOUZI Fatima

EL-HAGE Sahar

ENDO Miwa

ENGLISH Michael E.

ENOCQ Isabelle

ENOSAWA Yumi

ERNEST Katleen

ESHLER Valli

ESPAGNE Valerie

ESPOSITO Corinne

ESTIENNE Jerôme

EVANGELISTA Federico

EVANS Graham

EVRARD Brigitte

EVRARD Jean-Jacques

EXPOSITO Sylvie

EYNARD Nathalie

FABREGAT Pierre

FADIER Christine

FAHR Alexia

FANTOU Michel

FARAH Patricia

FARCY Gerard

FARGE Bertrand

FARHI Sophie

FARNIER Françoise

FARRAR John

FAUCHON Laurence

FAURE Helene

FAUX Catherine

FAVIER Agnes

FEKETE Dante

FELDHEIM Joanna

FERRANDON Agnes

FERREIRA Manuel

FERT Julien

FERTE Pasccale

FEUILLADE Sophie

FEVRE Stephanie

FIGUEIREDO Rui

FILAINE Catherine

FILLEUL Sophie

FINET Catherine

FITZGERALD Laura

FLORES Gaelle

FLORES Gilbert

FLORES Michele

FONTAINE Patricia

FONTAINE Valerie

FORGET Corine

FORNACCIARI Brigitte

FORNS Yannick

FOUGNIES Bruno

FOULON Annie

FOURNIER Pascal

FRADIN Jean-Claude

FRANCES Bruno

FREAS Chris H.

FRENKIEL Christine

FRESON Janine

FRIC Bernard

FROIDEVAUX Jeanne

FRUSAWA Koichi

GABRIEL Cecile

GAEL Jose

GAINZASNI Isabelle

GALATEAU Ariane

GALESNE Jean-Louis

GALLAND Jacques

GALLIN-SOUSSAN Deborah

GALLOIS Nathalie

GAMBY Marie-Pierre

GAND Jacques

GANTNER Michel

GARBOWITZ Aviva

GARCIA Antonio

GARCIA-FONS Dominique

GARCIA-GOMEZ Patricia

GARNIER Beatrice

GAROCHE Sandrine

GARUA Dominique

GAUDIC Xavier

GAULIER Marion

GAUTHRON Julie

GAYNOR Rachel

GAZEL Stephanie

GELDER Claude

GELY Marie-Laure

GENDROT Clara

GENTILHOMME Eric

GEOFFROY Karine

GEOGHEGAN Bernie

GEORGES Florence

GEORGIANNA Michael

GERARD Christine

GERARD Florence

GERBAUD Delphine

GERBIER Bernard

GERHARDS Dana

GERMANO Francine

GERVAISE Valerie

GILBERT Dominique

GILOUPPE Geraldine

GIMENEZ Francis

GIRARD Michel

GIRAULT Nathalie

GIROD Florence

GIROUD Sybil

GIVELET Anne

GIVELET Edith

GIZARD Eric

GLAENTZLIN Genevieve

GOBE Gwenaelle

GOBE Marc

GOETEYN Saskya

GOLD Wendy

GOLDEN Kevin

GONNELLE Jean-Louis

GONSE Christine

GOODWYN Peggy

GORET Nicolas

GOSSEA Suzy

GOUDARD Alberic

GOUDOUX Christine

GOURLET Marie-Claire

GOZEL Melek

GRAZIANO Melissa

GREIFENBERG Valerie

GREINER Carolin

GREUVET Eric

GRIMOUD Dominique

GRIS Damien

GRIS CHATAIN Chantal

GROSMANGIN Romain

GROSSI Stephane

GROSSLERNER Fabienne

GROYAU Jean

GUEBJ Alexis

GUELMAU Marie

GUELMAU Pierre

GUEZO Françoise

GUIBOURGE Jerome

GUICHARD Pascale

GUIGUES Charlotte

GUILLEMET Tiphaine

GUINIC Laure-Helene

GURMANKIN Caren

GUYOT Nelly

GYFTOPOULOS Rena

HA Jinyoung

HABER Andre

HACKER Nathalie

HADJI Hamadi

HADJI Moustafa

HAICAULT Virginie

HAINAUT Laurent

HALD, Wendy

HALEPIAN Caroline

HALLEY DES FONTAINES Cecile

HAMAS Fadhila

HAMEAU Fabrice

HAMELIN Michele

HAMILTON, Charles

HAMILTON, Martin

HAMLET Danielle

HAN Jade

HAN Jung-Hae

HANDFORD Henrietta

HARNER Judd

HASBANI Elie

HASEGAWA Keiko

HAVARD Isabelle

HEILIGER Stephanie

HENIN Anne

HENNING Agathe

HENRI Jocelyne

HENRY Nicole

HENRY Olivier

HERMANT Vincent

HERMEL Benjamin

HERRMANN Delphine

HERSCU Philippe

HESMAN Randi

HEYMANN Laure

HIENARD Mathieu

HIGASHI Takanori

HIGGINS Catherine

HILLIARD Katherine

HIRN Christina

HIRST Ken

HO Eugene

HOFFMAN Melissa

HOFFMANN Gerhard

HOISLE Allen

HON Stephanie

HOPPER Susan

HORAK-ANSBERG Jean-François

HORIKAWA Satoshi

HOUSTON Lela

HOVARD William D.

HUANG Shii Ann

HUBERT Martine

HUGHES Joyce

HUGON Albane

HUMLEN Anneliza

HUNT Caleb

HURAND Marie-Lise

HURE Yves

HUTH Manuel

HUYNH Alphonse

HWANG Sally

HYE JUNG Eun

HYGRECK Tiny

HYMAN Jack

HYVRARD Colette

ICHIKAWA Orie

IKEDA Naoko

IP Fiona

IRACI Lucia

ISAACS Amy

ISOGAI Ayako

ISRAEL David

ISSET Patrick

ITAMANAKA You

ITO Chikanori

ITO Yukiko

IWASAWA Shigeki

JABBAD Mohamed

JABLONSKI Joann

JACKSON Julio

JACOBS Natalie

JACQUET Eric

JACQUET Veronique

JACQUIN Catherine

JADOUI Sadok

JAKO MICA Jaqueline

JANICOT Agnes

JANIEC Alexandra

JANKE Kathrin

JAOUL Veronique

JARMAN Jori

JAROSSAY Fabrice

JAVAUX Murielle

JEANTY Annie

JEDOUI Mohamed

JEHANNO SERREU Claire

JELLAOUT Malika

JENTGEN Frederic

JI Kelvin W.

JILLOT Annie

JIN UM Hye

JOHNSON Caroline

JOHNSON Marilyn

JOHNSON Thomas

JOLY Fanny

JONCHEAU Xavier

JORGE Maria da Luz

JOSSO Claude

JOUINEAU Christophe

JUNG PARK Hae

KAKIMOTO Koji

KAKON Ruben

KALINSKI Lydia

KAMEGAI Tsutomu

KARDOS Mareen

KARTAGENER Stacey

KASAKS Tara A.

KATZ Pierre

KAUFMAN Amy

KEITA-BRUNET Karim

KELLACHAN Joe

KEMOUN Brigitte

KENNEY Cheryl

KERMARREC Nolwenn

KEROULLE Gaelle

KESKES Imad

KESZEY Stephanie

KIKUCHI Koichiro

KIM HEE Young

KIRK Victoria

KIUCHI Yasuo

KLARITCH John

KLEK Annette

KNAGGS Michael

KOENIGSBERG Lisa

KOHN Julien

KONIK Corinne

KORNEGAY Jeffrey

KOTECHA Mona

KRAFFT Juliette

KU Kathleen

KUCHTA Bozena

KUEN Fung

KULCSAR Marie-Jeanne

KUNKEL Dawn

KURSUN Leyla

KUSHNIRUK Carol

KUSING Florence

KUSS Susan

KYOKO Kyoko

KYUNG CHUN Yun

LABENNE Claudia

LABILLE Marie-Laure

LADEUILLE Isabelle

LAFOND Colette

LAFORGE François-Xavier

LAGARDE Daniel

LAGERWEY Chloe

LAHALLE Delphine

LAI Helen

LAINE Ludovic

LAINEY NORBERTI Aline

LALANNE Sandrine

LALLI Gina

LALONDE Alexandra

LAM Hanh-Claire

LAMBERT Fred

LAMBLIN Christine

LANAY Marielle

LANFREY Benedicte

LANG Catherine

LANGE Kyla

LANGLOIS Gregg

LANGLOIS Sophie

LANNA Paolo

LANNEAU Philippe

LAQUAIRE Reine

LASTENNET Marie

LAU Belinda

LAVERGNE Didier

LAZARUS Norman

LE BARBE Noemie

LE BOLEDEC Monique

LE BRETON Annick

LE CAM Yannick

LE CANU Michel

LE DEROFF Valérie

LE GLAUNEC Valerie

LE HENAFF Ronan

LE MOUEL Veronique

LE NEVANIC Bernard

LE ROUZIC Florence

LECAM Annick

LECANU Florence

LECHERE Fanny

LECOULTRE Gwenael

LEDEZ Marine

LEE Derrick

LEE Gabriella

LEE Soo

LEFEBVRE Jean-Pierre

LEFEBVRE Virginie

LEGER Carole

LEGRAND Janine

LEGROS Karelle

LEHOUX Sebastien

LEJEUNE Veronique

LELLOUCHE Raphael

LELONG Evelyne

LEMAIRE Sylvie

LEMAITRE Sandrine

LEMARCHAND Francine

LEMEE Christine

LEMNEI Dragos

LEMPORTE Marie-Christine

LENDORMY Sophie

LEONARDI Jean

LEONG Angela

LEPRINCE Eric

LERAT Jean-Marie

LERIBON Pascale

LERIDON Severine

LEROUET Jean

LEROY Virginie

LESAGE-CHOPARD Florence

LESAUX Alain

LESCURE Emeline

LESERTEUR Christine

LESIEUR Claire

LEUNG Kitty

LEUNIS Patricia

LEURET Antoinette

LEVET Stephanie

LEVET-STENNE Emmanuel

LEVINE Peter

LEVINSON Gwenola

LEVY Pearl

LEVY Sara

LEWIS-CONLIFFE Erica

LEYMARIE Delphine

L'HOMME Sebastien

LHOMMET Paul

LHOTE Rejane

LI Veronica

LIANG Virginie

LIBSEKAL Missla

LIEBEL Kevin

LIEBERMANN Sophie

LIENARD Bruno

LIEVORE Christine

LINDSEY Lashawn

LINES James

LIRITIS Elisabeth

LIU Joy

LO Yvonne

LOBFOY Prisca

LOCQUENEUX Gwenaelle

LOEW Edith

LOEW Emilie

LOK Francesca

LONGCHAMP Sylvie

LONGUEVILLE Remy

LOO Marie-Christine

LOPEZ William

LOZBER Odile

LU Wendy

LUCIUS Christophe

LUGO Nelson

LUMAX Stanley

LUNEL Vincent

MA Edwin

MAC CARTHY Catherine

MAC CATO Jerry

MADDENS Catherine

MADINIER Sylvie

MAEGLI Anne

MAGNIER Hubert

MAHE Caroline

MAIDENBERG Laure

MAIRE Pierre-Emmanuel

MAITRE Jerome

MALDAN Katrine

MALEK Diana

MALET Laurence

MALLET François-Marie

MAN So Fan

MANACHES Sophie

MANCHA Amy

MANDAGAROUD Arnaud

MANIEI Nazak

MANZONNI Fernando

MANZONNI Frederique

MARANO Isabelle

MARCADE
Marie-Anne

MARCHAIS
Stephanie

MARCHAL LEIBU-
NOGUIH Marion

MARGUET
Françoise

MARIE Bertrand

MARIN Michel

MARIN Pierre

MARIONVALLE
Sandrine

MARKS Esther J.

MAROTZ Leslie

MARQUETTE
Corinne

MARRA
Marie-Christine

MARTIN Corinne

MARTIN Jose

MARTIN Karine

MARTIN Olivier

MARTIN Priscilla

MARTIN Rabisha

MARTINEZ
Francisca

MARTINS Agostino

MARTON Fabienne

MASSE
Marie-Pierre

MASSE
Pierre-Frederic

MASSELOT Agnes

MASSENAT Alice

MASSEY Scott

MASSON
Benedicte

MATA Marine

MATHIEU Aline

MATSUDA Megumi

MATTERA
Jean-Paul

MAUFRAND
Yannick

MAUVIEUX
Jean-Claude

MAUVIGNIER
Danielle

MAY Eric

MAYEN Andree

MAYNE Michelle

McCOLLUM Walter

McCORMACK Josh

McDANIEL
Tabanitha

McMENNAMIN
Deirdre

McWHINNEY
Susan

MEGRAT Xavier

MELETT Patrick

MELIN Jean-Marie

MELINDA Alonso

MEMPONTE
François

MERCADO
Santiago

MERCIER David

MERCIER Philippe

MESCHINO
Florence

MESNIER
Dominique

MESROBIAN
Jean-Alain

MEUER Mary

MEYER Sophie

MEZEY Melinda

MILHAUD Antoine

MILLER Elly

MILLET Pierre

MILLEY Mike

MILLIGAN Judith

MIN Alexandra

MINEUR Etienne

MIRA Mercedes

MIRAL PERRONY
Jerome

MIROUZE Monique

MITCHELL Brenda

MIURA Izumi

MOK KIM Seung

MOLLET François

MONGES Alain

MONNIER Mirene

MONVOISIN
Maryse

MOREAU Delphine

MOREAUX-NERY
Sylvie

MOREL Nadine

MORETTI
Veronique

MORICHAU-
BEAUCH Patrice

MORIN Gerard

MORIYAMA Miki

MORO Marc

MOUKRIM Aziz

MOULEDOUS
Vanessa

MOULIN Caroline

MOURGUE
Monique

MOURIAUX Marie

MOUTON Laurence

MOY Spencer

MUFLARZ Florence

MULLER Laurent

MULLOY Trish

MURPHY Julie

MURRAY Nadia

MUSARD Ghislaine

NABI Ghalta

NACHTOMI Abigail

NADEAU Renee

NAHALKE Suzanne

NAILLON Jane

NARBONNE
Philippe

NASELLI Pascale

NAVARRO Frederic

NAZARIAN
Fabienne

NEAL Joe

NESSON Didier

NEVIN Catherine

NG Cleopatra

NG Grace

NG Liver

NICASTRO Dean

NICHOLAS
Susan L

NICOL Chantal

NICOL Françoise

NICOLE Virginie

NIETO Nathalie

NIEVES Nancy

NIEVES Robert

NIJIMA Nobuhiko

NITOT Dominique

NOBLESSE Franck

NOCELLA Corinne

NOEL Benedicte

NOEL
Jean-François

NONNON Isabelle

NORGUET
Françoise

NOTEBAERT
Françoise

NOURGIERS
Marcel

NOUZILLE
Emmanuelle

NOVAK Geraldine

NUNES Jack

NUNES Maria
Valentina

O'DONAHUE Sam

OHANESSIAN
Chantal

OKAMOTO Akiko

OKAWA Akiko

OLIVIER Christelle

OLLER Mark

OLSON Kerri

OLSON Kristin

OMURO Yohei

ORDANO Franck

ORIEUX Philippe

ORNE Sarah

ORTIZ Antonio

ORTOLAN Valerie

OSEN Sharon

OSORIO Maria

OSTROWETSKY
Claude

OUDOT Dominique

OUHAYOUN
Raymonde

OULERICH Sylvie

PACHOLSKY Andre

PACTEAU Sylvie

PAES Cesar

PAISY Solange

PALLIGIANO
Christian

PAPAZIAN Edouard

PAPAZOGLOU
Frederique

PAPIN Vincent

PAQUIN Marianne

PARC Dominique

PARC Laurence

PAREL
Marie-Helene

PARENTE
Lawrence

PARIS Christiane

PARISOT
Dominique

PARJADIS Valerie

PARKIN Paul

PARRAUD Florence

PARRAUD
Françoise

PARSY Solange

PASCAL
Anne-Marie

PASCAL Brigitte

PASCALIE Olivier

PASQUET Isabelle

PASQUINI
Jacqueline

PASSOS Emilia

PASTEAU Catherine

PASTISSON Benoît

PASTOR Veronique

PATTE Olivier

PAUL Sylvie

PAULNACK Greg

PAYNEayne,
Lucinda

PECHARD
Elisabeth

PEDREIRA
Norberto

PEET Renee

PENTO Alain

PERCY Jennifer

PERES Christophe

PERGAMENT
Patricia

PERONI Danelle

PERONNY Jerome

PERRET Isabelle

PERRET-GENTIL
Franck

PERRIER Christine

PERRIER Dridda

PERRIGO Nicole

PERROT Blandine

PERRUCHOT Anne

PETERSON John

PETRUS Isabelle

PEYRON Catherine

PEYRUSEIGT
Isabelle

PEZET Philippe

PHILPPON
Fabienne

PICARD Caroline

PICARD
Jean-Michel

PICHERIN Hugues

PIEDALLU Martine

PIERRE Florence

PIERRON Noelle

PIGEAUD Richard

PINAUD Virginie

PINEIRO Gloria

PINTADO Catherine

PIQUET Nathalie

PISANO Alexandre

PLANCHAIS
Gerard

PLANTE Gilles

PLAYER Thomas
Brett

PLISSONIER
Vincent

PLOSCOWE Lauren

POIGNARD Etienne

POLLACK Lucinda

POLO Sylvie

POMMEZ
Alexandra

PONS
Jean-Emmanuel

PONS Sophie

PONSAR Mayi

PORCELLA Cara

PORTNOY Eugene

PORTZ
Jean-Jacques

POUHYET
Stephane

POUILLON Josquin

POULAIN Nathalie

POULET Bernard

POUX Michele

PRAT Loic

PREVOT
Marie-Helene

PRIM Jacques

PRIVAT Sylvia

PRIVAT DE
FORTUNIE Karine

PUGADE
LORRAINE Xavier

PUGH Robin

PURDY Robert

QUELEN Marc

QUENTIN Sandrine

QUERE Sylvie

QUILICI Dominique

QUILLIO Beatrice

QUIROGA Maria

RABANT Karine

RABELO Mercedes

RADOMSKI
Guillaume

RAJAUT Muriel

RAMON Maldonado

RAMPACCI
Graziella

RAVELLY Nicolas

RAVET Claire

REFFET Helene

REICHLE Jana

REIN Frederic

REISCHLE Karl

REMIER Ghislaine

REMY Edith

REMY BOUTANG
Delphine

REMY NERIS
Jean-François

RENAUD
Anne-Catherine

RENAUD Luc

RENAULT Magali

RENDU
Emmanuelle

REPESSE Jean

RESTREPO
Corinne

RESTREPO
Federico

RESTREPO
Nathalie

REVET-STENNE
Emmanuel

REYNES Françoise

RIBAUD
Anne-Frederique

RIBES Christiane

RICHARD
Jean-Michel

RICORNEAU
Francis

RICOUT Christiane

RINA Céline

RIOU Magalie

RIQUEZ Olivier

RIVOALION
Dominique

ROBAT
Léon-Charles

ROBBINS Ali

ROBERT Anne

ROBERT Catherine

ROBIN Odile

ROBINSON
Timothy

ROCHE Jean

RODRIGUES
Natalie

RODRIGUEZ
Christine

ROGEAU
Marie-Christine

ROHL Vanessa

ROLANDO
Marie-Helene

ROMAN Manuel

ROMIEUX Carole

RONTEIX Valerie

ROSANVALLON
Benjamin

ROSENHEIM Cindy

ROSS Allison

ROSSI Ariane

ROSTAING Michel

ROUDOT Florence

ROUGERIE
Delphine

ROUSSEL Valerie

ROUSSI Anne-Lise

ROUX Catherine

ROUXEL Anne

ROY Beatrice

ROYER
Anne-Sophie

ROZE
Jean-François

ROZENBERG Lydia

RUAULT Sophie

RUBIN Delphine

RUDEL Roger

RUGGERI Angelo

RUMTHARWAN Sarmonk

RUTTER Harriet

RYKE Veronike

SACCOMANNO Barrie J.

SAIB Valerie

SAINSON Elise

SAINT ABLEAU Dominique

SAINT AVIT Lucille

SAITO Nobuko

SALEM Coralie

SALVADO Jean-Baptiste

SALVO Maria

SAMBERG Todd

SAMSON Angela

SANDOZ Chantal

SANS Andrea

SANTIAGO Erica

SANTIAGO Michelle

SARRAY Charlotte

SARRAZIN Melissa

SARRE Adreana

SARTHOUT Claire

SASAKI Yoko

SAUER Elif

SAULEAU Marie-Laure

SAUVET-GOICHON Sabine

SAUZAY Pascaline

SAUZEAU Christine

SAVAGLIO Nadege

SAVARY Claudine

SAVARY Olivier

SAVITT Nazak

SCEILI Kimberly

SCHATZLE Sylvie

SCHELLINO Alexandre

SCHMIDT Sylvie

SCHNAPP Daniele

SCHNELWAR Karen

SCHOLL Rory

SCHOLL Vivian

SCHROEDER John

SCHUBERT Isabelle

SCHWAB Olivier

SCIORATO Christine

SCOFFONI Nicole

SCOTT Molly

SEBAN Danielle

SEEMULLER William

SEGAL Dafna

SENTIS Marie-Helene

SERRA Elisa

SERRA Maria

SERRADJ Amina

SERRAT Eleonore

SERRAT Maurice

SETON-MARSDEN Aladair

SEYS Clementine

SHERR Leslie

SHIPOM Garris

SIEMBORA Theresa

SIK LEE Young

SILHOUETTE Virginie

SILLS Brett

SIMON Isabelle

SIMON Jennifer

SIMONET Christine

SIMONET Laetitia

SIMONETTA Brigitte

SINCLAIR Angus

SKIBINSKI Kristin

SKROTZKY Veronique

SLADDEN Clementine

SLUSHER Richard

SMIR Yasmina

SOCHOR Krista

SOFIANOPOULOU Christiana

SOLANA Linda

SOLNICA Odile

SOLNON Karine

SOLO Florence

SOMMET Danielle

SOMPHANH Bountoum

SONKIN-SAMBO Nicole

SONNET Pierre

SONNINO Yves

SOOK PARK Young

SOPHIANO Christiana

SORENSEN Pernille

SOULIER Yannick

SPENCER Dorothy

SPIEGEL Bernard

SPINELLI Alexander

SPOHR Brynne

SPRIET Therese

STEIN Lenny

STEINBERG Bruce

STELLAMANS Nike

STINGO David

STOJADINOVIC Dusica

STOJISAVIJEVIC Michel

STOLZ Emmanuel

STOMER Marcus

STOUT Craig

STREIFF Emmanuel

STRINGER Dominique

SUCCO Muriel

SUDOUR Emmanuelle

SUZANNE Christine

SUZUKI Miho

SWAN Anne

SWANSON Cheryl

TAIBI Myriam

TAILLET Genevieve

TALBOT Claude

TAM Carina

TANIGUCHI Asuka

TAPIA Christie

TARFAOUI Yahia

TASSEAUX Valentin

TECHER Maggy

TEINTURIER Axel

TERRASSON Beatrice

TEYSSECHE Fabienne

TEYSSIER Fabienne

TEYSSIER Muriel

THAM Elaine

THERIN Anne-Sophie

THEVENOU Corinne

THIBAUD Agathe

THIEL Colette

THIERROT Carole

THIOS Katherine

THIRY Claude

THOMAS Carol

THOMAS Philippe

THONNAT Elvire

THORAVAL Isabelle

THOROTON VICKERS Paul

TIBERGHIEN Gilles

TIGHE Deirdre

TIRARD Guillaume

TIRARD Veronique

TISON Claire

TITRE Helene

TOBIAS Odile

TOIRON Sandrine

TOLEFANO Annabelle

TOMASSI Eduardo

TONNEL Isabelle

TOPART Sandrine

TOPART Sylvie

TORRES Aurelie

TORRONTEGUI-SALAZAR Maria

TORRONTEGUY Anna

TOUREN Gerard

TOUSTOU Michel

TOUTOU Eric

TOWNES Debra

TRAMARD Nadine

TRAN-DINH Veronique

TRAUTHANH BIUH Mirh

TREGOUET Marie-Christine

TRIFOL William

TROJANI Nathalie

TRUFFAUT Caroline

TUZZI Alberine

UBA Laurence

ULLENBERG Frances

UNTERBURGER Thomas

VAGNAUX Alexandra

VAILLANT Pascal

VAILLON Olivier

VALAIS Catherine

VALAIS Guy

VALCARCE Jean-Louis

VALLA Charles

VALLA Clement

VAMER-MULIOT Gerald

VAN DEN BROCK Christine

VAN ERTVELDE Richard

VAN ESPEN Frederique

VAN RIEZEN Federico

VANNEUVILE Benoit

VANRECHEM Anne

VARGAS Jose

VARIGAULT Anne-Marie

VASSEUR Christine

VAYSSIERES Zoe

VAZQUEZ Lydia

VENET Florence

VENNING Lisa

VERBEEK Marianke

VERDIER Sylvie

VERGNERES Sandrine

VERICEL Marc

VERNET Caroline

VERNET Isabelle

VERNIER Daniel

VERRERI Vito

VICE Christopher

VICKERS Paul

VIENNE Veronique

VIGNERON Mathilde

VILLARD Catherine

VILLECOURT David

VINCENT Caroline

VINCENT Eric

VISCONTI Philippe

VIVES Pierre

VIVIER Isabelle

VOLVAU Annie

VOYER Annabelle

VUILLEMIN-PER-RIER Florence

WAGNER Barbara

WAGNER Cecile

WAGON Virginie

WAHL Laurence

WAHL DIT BOYER Guillaume

WAKESHIMA Satoru

WANG Ying

WARNER Mark

WATTEL Gildas

WEIDEL Franck

WEISBERG Jamie

WEISZ Yolande

WELLOTT Leslie

WHITE Rhea

WIHAME Fatima

WILDER Aimee

WILKINS Rondell

WILLER Charlotte

WILLIAMS Eric

WISDOM Colleen

WOLF Alexandra

WOLFF Nathalie

WONG Herbert

WONG Peggy

WOOD Jessica

WOSILIUS Jacquelyn

YACOUB Sonia

YAEGER Leyden

YAKHONTOFF Nicolas

YAMADA Yohei

YAMPOLSKY Hannah

YAM-VOLLET Sealine

YEUNG Adam

YEUNG Paul

YI Lori

YOSHIKAVVA Mami

YOUNG Jennifer

YOUSTIAKOV Laurence

ZAGALA Myriam

ZAPATA Maritza

ZARAGOZA OLIVIERBALAY Virginia

ZECCHINETTI Florence

ZEE Karen

ZEMMOUR Danielle

ZENK Sabrina

ZHANG Amy

ZIEBA Ghislaine

ZINGUILLI Muriel

ZOGO MASSY Yolande

ZORN Yvon

ZORRILLA-SAN MARTIN Alicia

ZUZA Renée

DIRECTORY DESGRIPPES/GOBÉ

Air France
Roissy-Charles de Gaulle Airport
Paris, France
www.airfrance.com

Albertville Olympics

Amélie
Paris Croissant Co., LTD
5F Hwa-jung Bldg.
Shinsa-Dong, Kangnam-ku
Seoul, 663-14, Korea

Ann Taylor Stores Corporation
7 Times Square
New York, NY 10036 USA
www.anntaylor.com

America Online
22270 Pacific Boulevard
Dulles, VA 20166 USA
www.aol.com

AOL Red
AOL LLC
22000 AOL Way
Dulles, VA 20166 USA
www.aol.com

Aqua Samoa
Aggie Grey's Resort,
near the wharf at Mulifanua
Mulifanua, Upolu, Samoa
www.aquasamoa.com

Aquarius
Coca Cola Services S.A.
Chaussee de Mons 1424
1070 Brussels, Belgium
www.cocacola.be

Avalon
47 W. 20th St.
New York, NY 10011 USA

Bath and Body Works, Inc.
7 Limited Parkway East
Reynoldsburg, OH 43068 USA
www.bathandbodyworks.com

Bonactive
Coca-Cola China Limited
18/F, Lincoln House, Quarry Bay
Hong Kong
www.coca-cola.com

Boucheron
Paris, France

Brooks Brothers
346 Madison Avenue
New York, NY 10017 USA
www.brooksbrothers.com

CJ Corp.
500, Namdaemoonro
5-GA, Jung-Gu
Seoul, 100-802, Korea
english.cj.net

Clear
Verified Identity Pass, Inc.
1270 Avenue of the Americas,
Suite 508
New York, NY 10020 USA
www.verifiedidpass.com

Club Med
11 rue de Cambrai 75019
Paris, France
www.clubmed.com

Coca-Cola
One Coca-Cola Plaza
Atlanta, GA 30313 USA
www.coca-cola.com

Danone
130 rue Jules Guesde
Levallois Perret Cedex 92393
France
www.danone.com

Dassault Falcon Jet Corporation
Teterboro Airport
Box 2000
South Hackensack, NJ 07606 USA
www.dassaultfalcon.com

Domtar
395 de Maisonneuve Blvd. West
Montreal, Quebec H3A 1L6
Canada
www.domtar.com

EFD
Maccabi Building Room 2238
1 Jabotinsky St.
Ramatgan, Israel
www.efd.com

Eastern Mountain Sports
1 Vose Farm Road
Peterborough, NH 03458 USA
www.ems.com

Estée Lauder Companies
767 Fifth Avenue
New York, NY 10153 USA
www.esteelauder.com

Evian
22 avenue des Sources 74500
Evian, France
www.evian.com

Fauchon
26 Place de la Madeleine 75008
Paris, France
www.fauchon.com

S.A. Les Parfumeries Fragonard
20 boulevard Fragonard 06130
Grasse, France
www.fragonard.com

The Gillette Company
Prudential Tower Building
Boston, MA 02199 USA
www.gillette.com

Godiva Chocolatier, Inc.
Campbell Soup Company
1 Campbell Place
Camden, NJ 08103 USA
www.godiva.com

Les Grands Montets
Compagnie du Mont Blanc
35 Place de la Mer de Glace 74400
Chamonix, France
www.compagniedumontblanc.fr

Imperia
Russian Standard Vodka (USA)
Company
1395 Brickell Avenue, 8th Floor
Miami, FL 33131 USA
www.russianstandard.info

Johnnie Walker Stores Inc.
234 West Wisconsin Avenue
Milwaukee, WI 53203 USA
www.johnniewalker.com

Johnson & Johnson
One Johnson & Johnson Plaza
New Brunswick, NJ 08933 USA
www.jnj.com

Kenzo Parfums SA
54 Rue Etienne-Mariel
75002 Paris, France
www.kenzo.com

LIME
10 East 40th Street
New York, NY 10016 USA
www.lime.com

Musashino University
1-1-20 Shin-machi
Nishitokyo-shi
Tokyo, Japan
www.musashino-u.ac.jp

Natura Cosmeticos S/A
Rod. Regis Bittencourt, Km 293
Itapecerica da Serra
São Paulo, Brazil
www.natura.net

Payless ShoeSource, Inc.
3231 SE 6th Avenue
Topeka, KS 66607 USA
www.payless.com

Peltier

Pernod-Ricard
(formerly Allied Domenecq)
100 Manhattanville Road
Purchase, NY 10577 USA
www.pernod-ricard-usa.com

Procter & Gamble
One Procter and Gamble Plaza
Cincinnati, OH 45202 USA
www.pg.com

Rakuten Eagles
2-11-6, Miyagino, Miyagino-ku
Sendai, Japan
www.rakuteneagles.jp

Starbucks Coffee Company
2401 Utah Avenue South
Seattle, WA 98134 USA
www.starbucks.com

Tour de France

Travelocity
8750 N. Central Expressway,
    Suite 1200
Dallas, TX 75231 USA
www.travelocity.com

VP Bank
Aeulestrasse 6
FL-9490 Vaduz Liechtenstein
www.vpbank.com

Weight Watchers International
11 Madison Avenue, 17th Floor
New York, NY 10010 USA
www.weightwatchers.com

World Golf Hall of Fame
PGA Tour
112 PGA Tour Road
Ponte Vedra Beach, FL 32082 USA
www.golfweb.com

World March
Moonstar
www.worldmarch.com

XL Lounge
357 West 16th Street
New York, NY 10011 USA